TEXAS
AFTER
SPINDLETOP

THE SAGA OF TEXAS SERIES
Edited by Seymour V. Connor

THE SAGA OF TEXAS, 1901=1965

TEXAS
AFTER
SPINDLETOP

by SETH S. McKAY
and ODIE B. FAULK

Illustrated by Joe Nerlinger

Steck-Vaughn Company
Austin, Texas

47508

About the Author

SETH S. MCKAY received B. A. and M. A. degrees from the University of Texas before going
to the University of Pennsylvania where he received his Ph. D. degree. He has taught at Texas
Technological College for more than thirty-five
years. Among his published works are *Texas
Politics, 1906-1944; W. Lee O'Daniel and Texas
Politics, 1938-1942;* and *Texas and the Fair Deal,
1945-1952.*

ODIE B. FAULK received B. S., M. A., and Ph. D.
degrees from Texas Technological College. He
has taught at Texas A & M University and has
been assistant editor of *Arizona and the West.* He
is author of *Tom Green: A Fightin' Texan* and
The Last Years of Spanish Texas and co-author of
Government by the People and *Lancers for the
King.*

Library of Congress Catalog Card Number 65-22122
Copyright © 1965 by Steck-Vaughn Company, Austin, Texas

Preface

Ralph Waldo Emerson once wrote: "There is properly no history, only biography." And indeed the statement is true, for the past is nothing more than a combination of the many lives that have been lived. But this means the writing of a history of twentieth-century Texas is a difficult one, for the Lone Star State has increased rapidly in population until it numbers more than ten million within its borders. And the recent era has produced some of the most colorful and diverse characters of its long history.

Compounding the difficulty of the historian who would write a history of recent Texas is the paucity of biographies of these men who have led the state, the lack of availability of personal papers and correspondence, and the scarcity of memoirs, diaries, and journals. Consequently the great bulk of the research behind this book was done in the files of the state's leading newspapers and in federal and state publications.

The research and the synthesis of the events of this era were first done in Professor McKay's numerous publications on modern Texas—mentioned in the "Point of View" at the end of the volume. As senior author, Dr. McKay then prepared a draft for the present work, and Dr. Faulk revised and re-drafted the text, after which it was reexamined and pruned slightly by Dr. McKay. Thus the authors hope that they have solved the problem of historians of the recent period since the basis for the text rests firmly on recent reports, and the story has passed through several distillations.

Incomplete as it is in many respects, and largely a political history, the authors believe, nevertheless, that this narrative will provide a clear view of recent times in Texas.

SETH S. McKAY
ODIE B. FAULK

Table of Contents

1

Spindletop — and After

NEW YEAR'S DAY had come and gone more than a week before, and by January 10, 1901, the people of Beaumont had accepted the fact that the twentieth century had arrived at last. But during the early morning hours that day few if any of the nine thousand residents of the little Southeast Texas town could tell any difference between the new century and its predecessor as they went about their usual business. William McKinley was still president and they assumed he would be for another four years; John Philip Sousa was scheduled to lead a concert in the town that night; and the Chamber of Commerce still talked of the need of attracting industry to the area.

It was not quite eleven o'clock when Captain Anthony B. Lucas stepped from his buggy and entered Louie Mayer's store on Crockett Street. After greetings had been exchanged, Louie undoubtedly asked with a smile of skepticism about the progress of the oil well that the captain was drilling a few miles away at a place known locally as Spindletop. The two were chatting amiably when the telephone rang at 11:15. It was Mrs. Lucas, who excitedly asked the storekeeper for her husband.

"Anthony," she cried when he answered, "something awful has happened! The well is spouting!"

Without another word, Lucas dropped the phone and ran from the store to his buggy. He whipped his horse to a fast pace down Park Street, turned onto Highland Avenue, and raced out of town. As he neared the crest of a hill overlooking the well site, he saw the cause of his wife's excitement. From the well floor a steady column of black liquid was shooting more than a hundred feet into the air and cascading over his small wooden derrick. A heavy sulfuric odor hung in the air and filled his nostrils.

The sight was so awe-inspiring that Lucas could hardly believe his senses. Could it be oil? Had his dream come true? Was this what he had labored for so long to find?

He was so excited by the possibility that the answer to his questions was "Yes!" that he decided the buggy was too slow. At the crest of the hill he jumped from the vehicle to cover the rest of the distance on foot. Instead, he stumbled, fell, and rolled down the hillside, finally coming to rest almost at the feet of Al Hamil, his chief driller.

"What is it?" he cried, fearing the worst, yet hoping for the best.

"It's oil, Captain Lucas, every drop of it!" Hamil assured him.

And oil it was—in such profusion and such quantity the world had never seen before. Little wonder that Lucas suffered a momentary confusion; even the largest wells in Pennsylvania were mere trickles in comparison to this dizzying spectacle. Fabulous Lucas No. 1, the Spindletop gusher, had blown in. It signaled the dawn of a new epoch in history—the Petroleum Age. The twentieth century had truly arrived.

Until that time, the oil industry was an infant. In Texas it was almost non-existent, although a quarter of a century earlier in Nacogdoches and somewhat later in other scattered places in the state there had been some small crude production from oil springs and shallow wells. What little petroleum had been brought to the surface had been retailed for lubricating and for medicinal purposes.

The first Texas oil boom occurred in 1896 at Corsicana, where by the turn of the century some three hundred wells had been drilled. During the four years of the boom there, over 800,000 barrels had been taken from the ground. The Lucas gusher at Spindletop spewed out that much oil in ten days! No one could have anticipated such unprecedented production, nor could anyone have predicted its effects on Texas or the world.

The Spindletop story, climaxed by the gusher of January 10, 1901, had actually begun nearly a decade earlier. Patillo Higgins had organized the Gladys City Oil, Gas and Manufacturing Company in Beaumont in 1892 in the wild hope of finding oil in a salt dome structure near town. Lucas, a mining engineer who had extracted sulfur from similar formations in Louisiana, became convinced of the prospects of oil at Higgins' location, took over direction of the operations in 1899, and doggedly persisted in attempts to pierce through a thick layer of quicksand which overlay the salt dome. After several futile trials, a new

At Spindletop

hole was spudded in on the little mound three miles from Beaumont in October 1900. Once again sand oozed into the hole faster than the drillers could clean it out. Lucas devised a new system of telescoping 12-, 10-, 8-, 6-, and 4-inch pipe into the hole, and the drilling crew labored exhaustingly to penetrate the "Gumbo" formation. On December 10 they reached the top of the salt dome and cased the sand out of the hole. Drilling into the rock commenced, but Lucas decided to shut down from December 24 to January 1 to give his tired workers time to rest. When they began again in the new year, they found the rock created different problems. A new drill bit was obtained, and on the morning of January 10 they began lowering it into the hole. Before the bit reached the bottom, however, a shower of mud and water erupted, throwing the bit and the seven hundred feet of drill pipe up through the rig, taking cable, pulleys, crown block, and all with it.

The drillers scampered to safety to await developments. Soon the well quieted, and they cautiously returned to clean up the derrick floor and repair the tackle. Suddenly, with a sharp report like the crack of thunder, a large volume of fluid mud shot out of the hole. Behind it with a deafening roar came gas under tremendous pressure, followed by heads of spurting oil. The noise and the flow increased, and, as the drill crew gasped and fled in amazement, rocks began hurtling hundreds of feet into the air. Finally came a strong, steady stream of oil, climbing twice the height of the derrick.

Chaos and pandemonium followed. Within hours hundreds of spectators rushed to the site to gaze at what was shortly labeled the "Eighth Wonder of the World." A fortune was spilling, uncontrolled, out of the bowels of the earth, constantly in peril of bursting into flame should a single carelessly ignited spark or flame touch it. In a feverous rush Lucas rapidly organized crews on 24-hour shifts to dig pits and drainage ditches, build firewalls, and keep the visitors safely back. Fifty men were needed to guard the well. Still others, using forty teams of horses, hurriedly threw up dikes and turned under the oil-soaked ground.

Working frantically for six days, the ingenious Hamil and his drilling crew devised a cap which they successfully forced over the powerful stream of oil shooting up out of the ground, diverting it instead out an eight-inch valve. The wild flow at last was under moderate control, but it still spat viciously from the valve in quantities conservatively estimated at 75,000 barrels a day. Lucas employed teams of men for days in building open pits to hold the flow of black gold.

Rampant speculation followed as hordes of visitors, promoters, and land speculators flocked to Beaumont and Spindletop. The hope of quick riches lured untold thousands to the scene. Special trains, crowded full, ran from every major city in Texas and Louisiana, and oil men hurried in from all parts of the country. Feverish trading and selling of land and leases ensued, not confined to "The Hill" (as Spindletop came to be known), but spreading out around Beaumont for a radius of nearly 150 miles. The late Boyce House, Texas author and oil editor, wrote the following vivid description for the *Southwestern Historical Quarterly* (July 1946):

> Beaumont looked like circus day, every day, with map vendors and peddlers of souvenir bottles filled with oil crying their wares; lease brokers shouted their "bargains" from boxes or wore signs in their hats as they mingled with the crowds that sometimes filled the street from building line to building line. Booths were built in the yard of the Crosby House, customers standing on the sidewalk. One tiny office was headquarters of five promotional companies—for the first nationwide speculation in oil stocks reached a "Mississippi Bubble" magnitude. The *Manufacturers' Record* published an estimate that the actual investment in the field was $11,000,000 but that the total capitalization of Texas oil companies was almost $232,000,000. Incidentally, some metropolitan newspaper writers gave the field a new name, Swindletop.
>
> Lines in front of cafes were a block long; grocery stores never closed; in fact, night and day meant little, for men would set out at midnight with lanterns to search for "gas bumps" and indications of oil. Unable to find a place to sleep, two men bought a mattress and placed it on the sidewalk on the principal street. A man, flipping

through a roll of $100 bills, came across a "ten-spot," which he tore up with the remark, "Small change, what are you doing here?" A woman who owned a little truck patch and a few hogs for which she hauled slop from town in two barrels on a dilapidated wagon leased her land for a fortune. A printer, who bought a lease and resold it the same day for a profit of $30,000, put on a celebration in which nearly all the printers in town joined; with a band, they went from bar to bar, drinking wine until the entire $30,000 was gone.

During the next year land within the vicinity of producing wells sold as high as a million dollars an acre, and land over one hundred miles distant at a thousand dollars an acre. On "The Hill" itself property was divided and subdivided as prices rose and drilling sites became exhausted. Blocks of six to eight hundred square feet (about the size of a large living room) sold for thousands of dollars, and since these blocks of land were scarcely larger than a derrick floor, additional space had to be rented on adjoining tracts for boilers and pipe.

Within a few weeks numerous wells were spudded in, and a mad drilling campaign continued for over a year. Wells on the 140-acre mound were drilled as close to each other as possible. So crowded were the derricks at the center of the field that drillers laid planks to walk from rig to rig above the greasy, slimy mud of the ground. Gushers followed one another in rapid succession. Some went uncontrolled for days; others were deliberately opened for the benefit of oil-crazed tourists. Together they constituted an increasing danger. On March 3 it finally happened—a gigantic fire swept across the open pits and burned for hours, consuming nearly a million barrels of oil and destroying considerable machinery and equipment before it could be controlled. Operators finally banded together and imposed voluntary regulations on the field for the sake of safety.

But no one seriously considered voluntary regulations limiting production. Before that first year had ended, Spindletop's gross output of over 3,500,000 barrels had startled industrial leaders from New York to Amsterdam, and the price of crude oil had dropped to three cents a barrel.

The next year, 1902, was even more fantastic. The field that sprang up around the well Lucas No. 1 yielded over seventeen million barrels. To make matters more serious, gusher production was found at other nearby salt domes, including Sour Lake and Batson. The economic turmoil that followed was actually of greater magnitude than the initial physical chaos.

To find additional uses of oil in order to build a bigger market became a matter of stark necessity for the hundred-odd producers at Spindletop. More oil was flowing out of that small hill than could even be stored, much less sold and used. The chief uses for petroleum at that time were lubrication and illumination; its use as a fuel was only in the experimental stages. Refineries, principally owned by John D. Rockefeller's Standard Oil syndicate, converted crude oil into kerosene and various grades of lubricating material. Practical internal combustion engines burning gasoline had just been invented during the previous decade, and oil from the Spindletop field was found to have such a strong asphalt base that it was believed unsuitable for so specialized a use. They would have to look elsewhere, they were told.

But it would burn—it would fuel a flame, and in specially adapted boilers it could turn water to steam, which in turn could be used to produce power. At Corsicana an enterprising engineer in 1898 had demonstrated that a coal-burning locomotive could be converted to use oil. His experimental model had been put to use on the run between Corsicana and Hillsboro. Texas railroad executives, therefore, were among the earliest to recognize the advantage of cheap oil, since their sources of coal were distant and the fuel relatively expensive.

Perhaps the first major line to begin converting its coal burners was the Houston and Texas Central; the Gulf, Colorado and Santa Fe bought a locomotive equipped with oil burners in June 1901; and the Southern Pacific instituted a program for the replacement of all coal-burning locomotives in its Atlantic Division on July 31, 1901. Both the Santa Fe and the Galveston, Harrisburg and San Antonio railroads soon adapted over two hundred engines for oil burning. Other lines, when they saw the advantages, followed suit. The Texas and New Orleans bought thirty-eight of the new engines; the Kansas City Southern, with a terminus at Port Arthur, ran forty oil burners onto its tracks; the International and Great Northern cautiously tested two converted locomotives with such conclusive results that it likewise made a complete switch; within a few years it was difficult to find a coal-burning engine in Texas.

If the new fuel was practical for locomotives, others reasoned that it must likewise be practical for steamships. By early 1902 the Shell Trading and Transport Company had three tankers operating on oil. In May of that year the United Fruit Company's converted *Breakwater* made a record-breaking run from New Orleans to Belize; the company officials were so impressed they promptly had three other ships converted and even built oil storage facilities in Honduras. Other steamship companies followed suit, and another major market was firmly established.

Indeed, in almost every application where coal served as a practical source of power, so could oil—and on the Gulf coast oil was far cheaper. One of the earliest uses found was for powering steam-driven irrigation pumps, and a number of Texas and Louisiana irrigation companies were among the first major purchasers of Spindletop's output. The American Brewery Company of Houston converted its five coal-burning boilers to oil; the Star Flour Milling Company of Galvestion began operating its fifty-horsepower milling machine from oil heat in 1901; and in the next twelve months a brick company at Gonzales, a hotel in Houston, a brewery in San Antonio, and an electric street railway company all installed equipment that used oil as a source of power. A year after Spindletop's discovery, a Texas geologist, Robert T. Hill, wrote that oil from the Lone Star State was "burning in Germany, England, Cuba, Mexico, New York and Philadelphia. By its energy steamers are being propelled across the ocean, trains are hastening across the continent, electricity generated and artificial ice frozen in New York, ores ground and stamped in Mexico, Portland cement manufactured in Havana, and gas enriched in Philadelphia."

While markets for the flow of black gold were sought and being developed, the producers moved rapidly to find an adequate means of storing the oil. Open pits were both insufficient and dangerous; so hundreds of wooden, cast iron, and even steel tank batteries were erected. Tank cars, also numbering in the hundreds, were run onto railroad lines, barges were floated down the Neches and Sabine rivers, oil storage tanks were added to freighters, and special oil transport ships were built. And still the oil flowed out of Spindletop and Sour Lake faster than it could be moved and sold.

By January 1902 a six-inch pipeline had been laid from the Spindletop field to the Neches River, two more to Port Arthur, and a fourth to Sabine. Additional lines from Beaumont to New Orleans, to Houston, to Galveston, and to other towns were planned. The practical use of relatively short pipelines linking the fields with coastal ports and shipping points cleared the way for another major development—the installation of refineries.

J. S. Cullinan built the first commercially practical refinery in Texas at Corsicana in 1898. In 1902 he organized the Texas Fuel Company (which later became the great Texas Company) and erected a refinery at Port Arthur. Already constructed and operating at that city was the refinery built by Captain Lucas' financial backers, two Pennsylvanians named John H. Galey and James M. Guffey. The Burt Oil Company erected one at Beaumont in 1902. Less than three years after the Spindletop gusher, more than ten million dollars had been invested in refineries in the region. Chemical analysis proved that the early fear of too much asphalt in the oil was a groundless one, and the Texas refineries were soon competing in every branch of the petroleum products market.

Permanent refineries and an expanding market for crude oil stimulated further exploration and increased wildcatting (drilling in an area where oil had not been previously found). By 1903, because of overdrilling and overproduction, the output at Spindletop and Sour Lake was dwindling noticeably; but in 1904 the Batson field reached a peak production of over ten million barrels. The next year a salt dome at Humble, in Harris County, was tapped and yielded over fifteen million barrels by the end of the year. Both the Batson and Humble fields continued to produce more than a million barrels annually for over a decade. Then Spindletop and Sour Lake showed signs of recovery, and neither dropped below the million-barrel mark until the 1920's.

While the wild search for oil continued in the Gulf coast salt dome areas, a crusty rancher, W. T. Waggoner, found it by accident on his Wichita County ranch in 1904 while drilling a water well. Despite the fact that the accident made him quite wealthy, Waggoner always complained that the oil production had ruined his ranch. Five years after the rancher's "unfortunate" discovery, the Electra field was opened in the vicinity. Other counties in North Texas were likewise soon in the midst of the oil boom.

The Petrolia field, also opened in 1904, lacked the enormous output of the salt dome fields, but its shallow depth made drilling easy and kept production costs small. At Powell in Navarro County another shallow field resulted from wildcatting in the Corsicana region, and exploration spilled over into Limestone County to open the Mexia field in the second decade of the century, although the boom that built Mexia's "Golden Lane" did not occur until 1921.

Early Texas oil production reached a peak of twenty-eight million barrels in 1905, dwindled to just under ten million in 1910, and then rose steadily nearly every year thereafter. New refineries were built at Fort Worth, Dallas, San Antonio, Houston, and Port Neches, and their total output expanded rapidly. During the period of contracting production between 1905 and 1910, a network of feeder pipelines was constructed to bring crude efficiently to the refining plants. Six- and eight-inch lines stretched for hundreds of miles to link the fields to the plants. One hungry refinery located at Fort Worth completed an eight-inch line to Oklahoma in 1908; oil had recently been discovered in the neighboring state at Glenn Pool.

By 1910 oil had become a big business in Texas. Energetic men and enterprising capital had made substantial permanent investments in the future of the state's oil industry. To a large extent the economic developments in Texas brought a financial diversification to the industry on a national scale at a time when it was badly needed in order to circumvent the emergence of monopolistic control. At least four major operating companies (together with a score of minor ones) grew out of the Texas boom and blossomed into world-wide competitive organizations.

The Gulf Oil Corporation's tap root is the Lucas No. 1 at Spindletop. Captain Lucas' supporters, Galey and Guffey, had obtained the money they risked at Spindletop from the Mellon brothers of Pittsburgh. To realize the potential of the fabulous gusher after it blew in, they needed to make further investments in production facilities. Again R. B. and A. W. Mellon advanced the necessary funds, and in May 1901 the J. M. Guffey Petroleum Company resulted from the Lucas-Guffey-Galey partnership. Of the 150,000 shares in the new company, one thousand went to Lucas, sixty-nine thousand to Guffey (Galey settled for a cash payment), twenty thousand were purchased by the Mellons, thirty thousand by other Pittsburgh capitalists, and the remaining thirty thousand by Carnegie associates. A few months later (on November 10, 1901) the same group of stockholders organized the Gulf Refining Company of Texas on the basis of a written agreement with the Guffey Petroleum Company. But soon the Guffey-Gulf companies had exhausted their funds, and amid decreasing production faced the problems of an inadequate refinery and a nearly disastrous delivery contract with the Shell Transport and Trading Company. W. L. Mellon, a nephew of the organizers and a man with experience in the oil business, was made executive vice-president of both companies with complete administrative authority.

Young Mellon soon demonstrated that the trust placed in him was merited. With additional capital and stable management, he revitalized the operations of the two companies. The delivery contract with Shell was bought back, and in 1903-1904 the Guffey-Gulf interests opened the Batson field, built a substantial refinery at Port Arthur, and ran pipelines to all the nearby producing areas. When Guffey retired in 1907, the two companies were united as the Gulf Oil Corporation.

Almost a twin to Gulf was the Texas Company; in fact, the name first selected by the Pittsburgh organizers of Gulf was "The Texas Refining Company," but they dropped it because another group had already incorporated under the name "The Texas Fuel Company" just a few months earlier. J. S. Cullinan, who entered the oil business in Pennsylvania and built Texas' first refinery at Corsicana, had founded the company in March 1901. Cullinan started in a small way; his firm was capitalized at only fifty thousand dollars and merely bought crude oil for transportation and resale. Former Governor James Stephen Hogg and the Hogg-Swayne syndicate put up $25,000 worth of oil properties, and Arnold Schlaet, representing John J. and Lewis H. Lapham, added $25,000 in operating funds. The Texas Fuel Company was ready for business on January 2, 1902.

On April 7 that year the company reorganized as the Texas Company and almost immediately began an extensive expansion program, including the erection of a large refinery at Port Arthur. Like the organizers of Gulf, Cullinan and his associates were badly hurt when the flow at the Spindletop field dwindled late in 1902. It was then that John W. (Bet-a-Million) Gates stepped forward to offer the funds necessary to develop the Texas Company's interests in the new Sour Lake field.

Gates had started down the road to fame and fortune as a barbed wire salesmen in Texas in the 1870's. His famous demonstration of the new fencing material in San Antonio made him and his company wealthy. In 1880 he organized his own fence company which he mushroomed in a series of fabulous business deals into the American Steel and Wire Company, participating later in the organization of the Republic Iron and Steel Company. No more interesting personality has ever played a role on the Texas economic stage; no better investment was ever made than Gates's Texas Company venture.

With $590,000 from Gates and about $400,000 from other sources, the Texas Company emerged from the Sour Lake boom in a strong position. Out of over two hundred companies organized immediately after the Lucas gusher, Gulf and "Texaco" alone developed over the years the gigantic proportions of independent major oil companies. Two others (the Magnolia Petroleum Company, a consolidation of Cullinan's Corsicana refinery with the Burt Refinery at Beaumont and several other companies, and the Humble Oil and Refining Company, which grew from independent operations in the Humble field) also became "majors" on a regional scale. Later they became affiliated with Standard Oil.

The establishment of these major companies in Texas typified what was probably the most profound effect of the early oil booms on the state—the introduction and investment of outside capital. Substantial investments in Texas oil lands, in refineries, and in pipelines and other oil-associated industries greatly broadened the state's economic base. In Texas the twentieth century blew in on January 10, 1901, instead of January 1.

2

Politicians and Issues, 1901-1913

SPEAKING BEFORE a gathering in Dallas in October 1911, Governor Oscar B. Colquitt commented, "We have only one political party in Texas, but there are enough . . . fights in that one for half a dozen." In one sentence, the governor had neatly summarized the situation in his state, for during the first dozen years of the twentieth century many personalities and issues continually divided the public into rival camps. Each issue, each politician, each struggle for office caused divisiveness, heated already inflamed tempers, and produced constant bickering.

Perhaps the most controversial figure during this period was Joseph Weldon Bailey, and the greatest issue was his honesty—or lack of it. Born in 1863, the son of a Mississippi saloonkeeper, Bailey as a teenager had attended several Southern colleges, finally receiving a law degree from Cumberland University at the age of twenty. The following year, like many another Southern youth, he decided that his future coincided with that of the Lone Star State and moved first to Sherman, then a few months later to Gainesville. As a small-town lawyer he soon entered politics. In 1887 he campaigned ardently for statewide prohibition. Before long he began his political apprenticeship in several minor offices. Apparently young Bailey learned quickly, for in 1890 he was elected to Congress from the Gainesville district. His ten years in the House of Representatives became another step in his political career. Bailey usually sided with William Jennings Bryan and Grover Cleveland in advocating lower tariffs and other progressive reforms, and as a rule he voted with the Southern Democrats and the agricultural interests. He favored the Spanish-American War, but opposed the imperialistic trends that followed. In the Fifty-fifth Congress he was a candidate for Speaker of the House and became the House Democratic minority leader. In 1900 his hard work was rewarded when he won election to the United States Senate.

After his entry into the upper house Bailey became more and more conservative, frequently voting with the Northern Democrats from the industrial states. He opposed most of the measures for which President Theodore Roosevelt worked, including the building of the Panama Canal by the United States. Soon he began to accept legal fees from the railroads and other large corporations, notably the Standard Oil Company and its various subsidiaries. Since the great corporations at that time were considered the natural enemies of the interests of the common people, there was a storm of opposition to him when it became known that he would seek reelection in 1907. Bailey, when he heard that certain Texans had started a move to unseat him, became greatly incensed. Before leaving Washington to begin campaigning, he stated that he was going to "drive into the Gulf of Mexico" all the "peanut politicians" who had spoken out against him. When asked about the possibility of his being replaced, Bailey said that if the legislature should do the unexpected and name the ablest of his opponents to the Bailey seat in the Senate, such opponent would fall so far short of filling the seat that he would "rattle around like a mustard seed in a gourd."

In July 1906 Senator Bailey was unopposed on the preferential ballot in the Democratic party's primary despite all the talk of unseating him, and at the state convention of that party following the voting he was unanimously declared the nominee. It appeared that Bailey had won a clear triumph over his detractors. But before the legislature, which met in January 1907, could act on the nomination, an inquiry into Bailey's relations with the great oil companies was started by Attorney General R. V. Davidson and aroused statewide interest. On the surface it appeared that Bailey had violated the ethics of his office, although there was nothing illegal about what he had done. Many prominent lawyers and other public men over the state argued in the press and in speeches that Bailey was guilty of consorting with the enemies of the people, that the senator had ceased to be an asset in Washington, and that he should not be reelected by the legislature despite the preferential primary result.

Bailey, assisted by the oil companies, defended his record; he and his friends argued that he had become the nominee of the Democratic party, that he had the right to practice law during his term as a senator, and that he

Joe Bailey

was a man of such remarkable ability that he should be
returned to the Senate by an overwhelming majority by
the legislature.

The most advertised charges against the senator were
alleged personal involvement with the Waters-Pierce Oil
Company and his acceptance of a retainer of $100,000 as
that company's counsel. He was also accused of similar
connections with the Standard Oil Company and with

the John H. Kirby lumber interests. In the fall of 1906 Bailey grew sufficiently alarmed at the turn of events in Texas and the widespread play the charges against him were getting in the newspapers that he returned to the state to defend himself. In numerous speeches throughout Texas he claimed that he had given legal services to his clients only when the Senate was in recess. He declared that every man had a right to support his family properly and that his work for the trusts had never conflicted with his duties in the Senate or his obligations to the people of Texas.

In the early years of the twentieth century the Texas antitrust laws were far more strict than those of the United States. In fact, by 1915 some 119 prosecutions were entered under the Texas antitrust laws, of which 84 were settled by compromise. The most publicized litigation of this nature concerned the Waters-Pierce Oil Company, a Missouri corporation doing business in Texas. In 1897 Attorney General M. M. Crane had brought suit against the company for violation of the Texas statutes and had secured a verdict in favor of the state which canceled the company's permit to do business inside the state. When the company appealed, the decision favoring Texas was upheld by the United States Supreme Court in a 1900 ruling. The company thereupon appealed to Bailey, who advised a new charter and was able to have it reinstated for business in Texas and Missouri in 1900. Missouri subsequently brought suit against the Waters-Pierce Company, showing that in 1900 the Standard Oil Company owned three thousand shares of Waters-Pierce stock, which was contrary to the sworn statements of the applicants when they petitioned for reinstatement in Texas. On the basis of the Missouri case, Attorney General Davidson filed suit in the fall of 1906 against the Waters-Pierce

Oil Company. He petitioned the court to cancel the company's permit to operate in Texas and to assess it approximately five million dollars in penalties.

The trial was one of the most famous in Texas court annals. During the course of the testimony taken, it came to light that Bailey had been advanced money during the election of 1900, funds that were termed a "loan," but which had never been repaid. When a decision in the case was finally reached, the company was found guilty of violating the Texas antitrust laws in its relations with the Standard Oil Company, was ousted from the state, and, after the verdict was sustained by higher court rulings, had to pay a fine of $1,808,483.30. The Texas property of the company was eventually sold at auction.

Thus it was that Bailey's association with the Waters-Pierce Oil Company became an issue in his campaign for a second term in the Senate. Bailey contended that he was completely innocent of wrongdoing and that he was the victim of an effort by William Randolph Hearst, the owner of a chain of newspapers, to destroy him and deprive the country of his great services.

To examine the Bailey record, the Texas legislature appointed an investigation committee; but before the committee had done much work that same legislature re-elected Bailey to the Senate by a large majority. The state Senate then exonerated Bailey, but the senator was still not satisfied. He announced that he would make the state delegation to the next Democratic national convention a test of his strength, that the people should select none but Bailey partisans as delegates, and that in such a manner Texans could manifest their trust in him. The special primary was set for May 1908; Texas was entitled to four delegates-at-large and four alternates. Cone Johnson of Tyler led the anti-Bailey forces in a bitter and exciting contest against the senator, but Bailey and his slate of delegates won by a large majority.

Texas voters were almost equally divided on the Bailey controversy; old friends had fallen out and even fought over the issue of the senator's honesty. Some seemed to consider Bailey a sort of political "saint" who could do no wrong, while others insisted that he was a representative of "predatory wealth" and had used his office as United States senator to secure more and larger legal fees. For nearly three decades after 1900, Texas voters were inclined to judge the qualifications of all aspirants for public office on the basis of whether the candidates favored or opposed Senator Joseph Weldon Bailey.

A similar situation existed during the same years about the issue of prohibition; Texans likewise measured all candidates for offices ranging from governor to constable on the basis of whether they were "wets" or "drys." On prohibition, as on Baileyism, the public was almost evenly split, although it could not be neatly classified into two opposing camps. Some who stood for temperance were against statewide prohibition; others favored local option and were opposed to statewide prohibition; still a third group favored total prohibition of the liquor traffic and believed that only a prohibitionist should hold public office in Texas.

Attempts to get a statewide ban on the manufacture, sale, or transportation of alcoholic beverages dated back to about 1870 when the United Friends of Temperance and its juvenile affiliate, the Bands of Hope, first made their appearance in the state. Their strength was increased in 1882 when the Woman's Christian Temperance Union began organizing in Texas. Together these elements mustered sufficient votes to persuade the legislature to enact in 1876 a local option law (providing that each county could determine for itself whether to be "wet" or "dry"), but the prohibitionists were still dissatisfied. A total ban on alcoholic beverages was their goal, and they would never rest until they saw their wishes become the law of the state.

In 1887 the legislature finally consented to submit to the people in the form of a constitutional amendment a prohibition measure. After a colorful campaign that even attracted national interest, 350,000 Texans went to the polls and turned down the amendment by a margin of nearly two to one. This contest temporarily slowed the prohibition drive in Texas; it was not until after the beginning of the twentieth century that the "drys" again regained their enthusiasm. At that time they began concentrating their efforts to secure local option elections and succeeded in adding many dry counties to their list in the northern part of the state. But they met with little success in East and South Texas where the "wets" had sufficient strength to defeat them.

The state's most exciting wet-dry contest, that of 1911, actually began with the governor's race in 1906. The candidates were Thomas M. Campbell, a known friend of ex-Governor Hogg and prohibition; Judge M. M. Brooks, a close friend of Senator Bailey and prohibition; Oscar B. Colquitt, well-known for his stand against all forms of prohibition; and Attorney General C. K. Bell, who was vague about his stand on the issue. With the aid of Bailey in the state Democratic convention, Campbell was nominated under the provisions of the new Terrell Election Law, and subsequently he was elected. In 1908, prohibitionist Campbell presented himself to the Democratic party for re-nomination; on the same primary ballot the voters were asked to state whether or not they favored prohibition. The prohibitionists won the election by a small margin, and Campbell was named the standard bearer of the party. However, when the legislature met in 1909, it ignored the "mandate" of the people to submit another prohibition amendment to the electorate.

In the Democratic primary in 1910 Oscar B. Colquitt, an anti-prohibitionist, was nominated. At the same time, by a thirty-thousand-vote majority, the electorate demanded that the legislature submit a prohibition amendment for their consideration. The legislature finally gave in and called the statewide test for 1911.

By that year Texas had 167 dry counties, 61 partially wet ones, and 21 totally wet, but in the wet counties were located the state's larger cities and the greatest voting strength. The cities were expected to give majorities against the proposed amendment, while the rural areas would favor it.

The ablest orators of the state, both for and against prohibition, spoke to crowds of thousands of listeners; rallies were held in all parts of Texas; large campaign funds were collected and expended; torchlight parades were featured; and the voters were kept excited for several weeks prior to election day. Leading speakers against the amendment, including Governor Colquitt, Secretary of State C. C. McDonald, several state senators, and Judge Nelson Phillips, warned Texans that should the amendment pass, new taxes would have to be voted to offset the loss of liquor revenues, the schools would suffer from the loss of tax monies, and the principles of individual freedom would be violated.

Taking the campaign trail for the prohibition advocates was an equally great array of speakers. Ex-Governor T. M. Campbell, Dr. George M. Truett, Cone Johnson, and Sam

Rayburn spoke of the evils of alcoholic beverages and urged the voters to adopt the amendment. The colorful "Cyclone" Davis and Baptist leader Dr. George Rankin waxed eloquent for the prohibition cause. The "drys" even sought to prevail upon William Jennings Bryan, three times a candidate for the presidency, to speak in Austin in their behalf, but he declined.

The election, conducted on July 22, drew more than twice as many voters as the 1908 gubernatorial contest. Almost half a million Texans went to the polls to fight one of the closest contests in Texas history. The "wets" won by a mere 6,297 votes (237,393 against prohibition, 231,096 for).

Despite the loss, the dry forces kept up the struggle, but they made little headway for the next four years. Not until 1915 did the tide of public sentiment begin to turn in their favor. It was that year that Attorney General Ben F. Looney uncovered evidence that the brewers had been violating the state's antitrust laws and the election code. Then in the 1917 impeachment trial of Governor James E. Ferguson, it came to light that the brewers had shown the discredited chief executive unusual and effective political favors. Finally, a decisive factor in the prohibitionists' drive was World War I, during which their goal took on patriotic overtones because the grain used in the manufacture of alcoholic beverages was needed for food. Also used by the prohibitionists in their effort to abolish the alcoholic beverage traffic was the widely held belief that young men who entered the military services should not be subjected to undue temptations. On April 15, 1917, this belief resulted in a law to forbid the sale of liquor within ten miles of any army post in the state.

Then at long last the "drys" achieved both in Texas and the nation what they had been seeking for so many years. A law of June 1918 closed all saloons in the state, and in July 1919 federal statutes prohibited the sale of intoxicating liquors anywhere in the country. The Eighteenth Amendment to the United States Constitution (the prohibition amendment), which was sponsored by Senator Morris Sheppard of Texas, went into effect on January 16, 1920. The "wets" had lost the battle—but not the war!

Other battles, just as hard fought and as lengthy as the wet-dry contest, did little to cool the heated tempers of the voters during the first years of the twentieth century. The political tranquillity at the turn of the century was a natural reaction to the progressive Hogg era and its reforms of the preceding years; for six years the state had a conservative government and relatively little political excitement. Other topics diverted the public attention—the Spanish-American War, the Galveston flood, and similar events. The two governors during those six years were elderly gentlemen: S. W. T. Lanham and J. D. Sayers. Both were ex-Confederates, both had been congressmen, and neither was widely known before seeking and obtaining the nomination of the Democratic party for the governorship.

The end of the period of political dullness came in 1906; Governor Campbell became involved in attempted tax reform, Baileyism divided the voters, and prohibition created a strong interest in politics. Up to the time of Campbell's administration the general property tax, which in most cases meant real estate tax, had provided the greater part of the state's revenue. Other forms of property, such as the railroad companies' rolling stock and ten thousand miles of track, were assessed more lightly than real estate, and most intangible property escaped the tax assessor-collector's notice.

Governor Lanham had called the attention of the legislature to the obvious taxation inequities that existed, and the session that met in 1905 passed new legislation to balance the burden. The intangible properties of railroads and certain other industrial groups were placed on the tax rolls by the 1905 law, which also placed a gross receipts tax on express companies, light and power companies, pipelines, sleeping-car companies, and telegraph and telephone companies. Two years later the legislature passed a "full rendition law" providing that all property should be rendered for tax purposes at its reasonable cash market value. It also provided that the governor, comptroller, and treasurer should constitute an automatic tax board with power to set the tax rate for general revenue and for schools.

Under these new laws, the total assessed value of property on the tax rolls went up from $1,200,000,000 in 1906 to $2,200,000,000 in 1908. Nevertheless the burden of taxation had not been shifted a great deal; real estate taxes still furnished two thirds of the tax money. Only after the development of the oil industry and the rise in automobile ownership did Texas come to rely heavily upon funds derived from taxes on natural resources and businesses.

Governor Campbell pursued a financial policy after 1907 which gained him both friends and enemies. He won a reputation for economy by vetoing some $1,700,000 from the 1909 appropriations bill, but his critics declared that most of the money had been earmarked for needed improvements. Campbell also made a fruitless effort to secure the passage of a state income tax law, which naturally angered still more people. He did get a small inheritance tax placed on the statute books; it produced a trickle of revenue and a flood of criticism. Campbell used his position on the automatic tax board to reduce the tax rate for 1910 after the Waters-Pierce Oil Company in 1909 paid its fine. Even this move, however, failed to satisfy Campbell's enemies. They declared the reduction was an obvious bid for popular approval and that the governor's successor would suffer because the tax rate would naturally have to be raised the following year.

Another piece of important legislation during the Campbell administration involved the reserve funds which insurance companies in Texas were required to maintain on policies in force in the state. The Robertson Insurance Law of 1907 required that at least seventy-five percent of these funds be invested in Texas securities and deposited in the state treasury. The Robertson law had a significant effect on the insurance companies, for prior to its passage they had invested less than three percent of the reserve funds in Texas securities. The insurance companies fought the bill bitterly; and when it passed twenty-one of them withdrew from the state, arguing that the legislation was unjust and unfair. Some of the companies that left later returned after the commissioner of insurance and banking modified certain of the regulations; all of them unsuccessfully continued their efforts to have the law repealed.

The nationwide Panic of 1907 caused minor financial distress in Texas because it led to a temporary shortage of currency and a brief limitation on depositor withdrawals by the banks. In an attempt to prevent such events from recurring and to provide relief to small depositors, the legislature in 1909 instituted an insurance program that covered bank deposits to a limited extent. However, the system later became unpopular because of the many bank failures in the early 1920's and was repealed in 1927.

The greatest reform in Texas during the first dozen years of the twentieth century was that which regulated the selection of candidates for public office and their election. The Terrell Election Law of 1903, named for its author, A. W. Terrell of Austin, endeavored to eliminate unfair and inefficient methods of voting, tried to formulate a code for regulating political parties' primary elections, and sought to end the lax practices that had crept into political conventions during the preceding fifty years.

Reforming the process of naming and electing officials proved even more difficult than it seemed at first glance, however, and Terrell decided it was necessary to do the job again. In 1905 he secured the passage of another law, also bearing his name, that began by repealing his first effort. In detail the new code stated who should be permitted to vote in primary and general elections, required candidates to file expense accounts within ten days after an election, provided that primary elections should be held by parties polling at least one hundred thousand votes in the last general election, specified regulations for the various party officials, and set the date for primary elections (the fourth Saturday in July of even-numbered years). It likewise provided that county and precinct party officials should be selected in the primary, and it left it to the county executive committee to decide if a second primary (runoff) should be held to decide between the two highest candidates in any or all races in which no one received a majority vote. Finally, it continued the poll tax, which had been established in 1902, as a requirement for voting.

From time to time there have been amendments to the Terrell Election Law to close loopholes in it or to cope with new developments. For example, in 1913 a law was passed requiring that a runoff be held to determine the party nominee for the United States Senate when no candidate received a majority in the first primary. In 1918 that provision was extended to other state and district races.

Following World War I the issue of race was injected into Texas politics; it had always been the policy of Texas Democrats to discourage Negro voting in the primaries, but a white primary law of 1923 would have excluded them altogether. After the United States Supreme Court held the law unconstitutional (*Nixon v. Herndon*, 1927), the legislature gave political parties the authority to exclude Negroes from membership through action of their state executive committees. That law was also declared invalid by the Supreme Court (*Nixon v. Condon*, 1932). Thereupon for several years Negroes were kept out of the primaries by the statement of each voter that he was "a white Democrat," but in 1944 the Supreme Court for a third time intervened, declaring that such a practice violated the rights of the Negroes and was unconstitutional (*Smith v. Allwright*). The Texas press after that decision forecast that thereafter there undoubtedly would be a large Negro bloc voting in every election, but such has not been the case. In the twenty years since the 1944 decision, the percentage of eligible Negroes who actually go to the polls has increased only slightly faster than the percentage of whites who participate.

Penitentiary and prison reform, long overdue, began during the period of the Campbell and Colquitt administrations. In 1908 and 1909 some of the big city newspapers in the state published long series of articles calling attention to the appalling conditions in the penitentiaries. These articles had the desired effect; the Thirty-first Legislature of 1909 created a committee to investigate the situation. The committee's report, released later that same year, caused a sensation over the state. It revealed that convicts had been shot or whipped to death for small offenses; that they were given unreasonable tasks and were severely punished for failure to accomplish them; and that food was poor, clothing inadequate, and sanitation worse. Financial affairs of the penal system were in confusion; the books were so poorly kept that they could not be audited.

The penitentiary system was the subject of much discussion in the 1910 political campaign; successful candidate O. B. Colquitt held that Governor Campbell was responsible for the neglect of the system and demanded reform, such as the abolition of the "bull-bat whipping strap." Following the election, Campbell called the legislature into special session, and several reforms were passed. The leasing of convicts for labor outside the system was abolished; a prison auditor was to be selected by the attorney general, comptroller, and state treasurer; management of the prison system was placed under the direction of three commissioners to be appointed by the governor; striped uniforms were to be abolished except for the worst class of prisoners; sanitation and medical service were ordered improved; and each convict was to be paid a small sum for his labor. Governor Colquitt, who had publicized the abuses during his campaign, found that most of them had been corrected by the time he took office.

Reforms in the penal system and the election code, the coming of prohibition, and the birth of the oil industry show that in the first years of the new century changes were commonplace in all aspects of life in Texas. The same was true about Texans on the national scene. Those whose political stars were just setting included ex-Governor James S. Hogg and ex-Senator John H. Reagan, both of whom had served Texas long and well. Hogg died in the spring of 1906, Reagan almost exactly a year earlier. Already on the national stage and gaining some prominence were Senators Bailey and Culberson and the enigmatic Colonel E. M. House. Newer men who made their first appearance during these years included Sam T. Rayburn, Senator Morris Sheppard, and the three Texans who served in the Woodrow Wilson cabinet—Albert Sidney Burleson, Thomas Watt Gregory, and David Franklin Houston.

Senator Charles Allen Culberson, a native of Alabama and a Texas resident for seventy years, was known in his earlier political career as a friend and lieutenant of Governor Hogg. He served as the state attorney general during the Hogg administration, then in 1894 with Colonel E. M. House as his campaign manager, defeated Thomas L. Nugent, the Populist candidate, for the governorship. He was reelected to a second term in 1896. Culberson was a "veto" governor who gained a reputation for honesty and for vigorous enforcement of the laws. One of his most controversial actions was his calling of a special session of the legislature in 1895 and securing the enactment of a special law banning a scheduled championship prize fight in the state.

In 1898 Culberson was elected to the United States Senate, where he served for twenty-four years. In Washington he put in long hours of hard work, and his fellow party members in the Senate recognized his abilities in 1907 by naming him minority leader. The following year he was considered for the Democratic nomination for the presidency. Noteworthy also was his service on the Committee on the Judiciary, of which he was chairman from 1913 to 1919.

During World War I his zeal and dedication to his work led him to overtax his strength, resulting in ill-health, but still he continued his labors. In 1922 Culberson failed to be renominated by the Democratic party mainly because he was unable to return to the state and campaign; a new generation of Texas voters had grown up without having seen or known him. After his retirement Culberson remained in Washington and died there on March 19, 1925.

The controversial Joseph W. Bailey went to Washington as junior senator from Texas in 1900 and was soon rated as one of the ablest orators and most impressive speakers of his time. Many of his audiences gladly stayed to hear him for two to three hours at a time. Tall and well-built, he was a man of impressive appearance and commanding voice. He became a personal friend of President William H. Taft and at one time declined an appointment to the Supreme Court saying candidly that he felt he was not suited to the duties of a judge. After his retirement from the Senate in 1913, he became overweight (scaling some 250 pounds); his bulk detracted from his speaking ability somewhat, but even so he was still greeted by some of the largest crowds ever to hear an orator in Texas. Bailey died on April 13, 1929, while participating in a law case in Sherman and was buried at Gainesville.

Edward Mandell House is still a controversial figure, one whose place in the history of Texas and the nation has been little understood. His biographer, Charles Seymour, insists that by his relations with Woodrow Wilson, Colonel House became the most influential man in America not holding elected office. Colonel House, the son of a wealthy banker and property owner, was born in Houston in 1858. At the age of seventeen he was sent to a private school in New Haven, Connecticut, where he became a close friend of Oliver Morton, son of the Indiana senator. Through the influence of the Morton family, House became widely acquainted with people of political promi-

E. M. House and Woodrow Wilson

nence and influence. He completed his formal education by studying at Cornell. In 1880 his father died, leaving House and his six brothers and sisters a considerable legacy in the form of plantations and other property. House married in 1881, spent a year traveling in Europe, and then settled in Austin because of his interest in politics.

Gradually he rose in political circles and in 1892 became campaign manager for James S. Hogg. He performed a similar service for the next three chief executives of the state—Culberson, Sayers, and Lanham. Given the title of colonel by Governor Hogg, House was a close friend of all four governors, especially Culberson. In 1911 the growing rift in the Republican party offered the Democrats an excellent chance of a presidential victory the following year, and it was about that time that House became acquainted with Woodrow Wilson. Mutual admiration and confidence developed between them, and an intimate friendship followed.

At the Democratic national convention in 1912 House was especially useful in giving his new friend the votes of the forty Texas delegates and in securing for him the support of William Jennings Bryan, both of which were instrumental in Wilson's nomination. In the ensuing campaign House acted as peacemaker, settling many squabbles between individual Democratic leaders. After Wilson became President, House refused any official appointment; instead he became the close confidant and principal advisor of the new chief executive.

House was one of the five American commissioners at the Peace Conference at the end of World War I. Perhaps his most outstanding achievement was selling to this body Wilson's Fourteen Points, which were designed to secure a lasting world peace. When Wilson returned to the United States during the middle of the conference, House remained as the personal representative of the President; later Wilson named House as his representative to London for the conference that drafted provisions for the operation of the mandate system set up by the Versailles Treaty.

Colonel House returned to the United States in the fall of 1919, but President Wilson had suffered a stroke and the two never met again. Although House had much less direct influence on public affairs during the last eighteen years of his life, he continued to correspond actively with his many personal contacts, among them the outstanding figures of the United States and the world. Leaders of the French and British governments consulted him, and his advice was valued by politicians in both United States political parties.

By 1932 Colonel House had regained a large measure of his former influence in the inner councils of the Democratic party. He supported the nomination of Franklin Roosevelt, but made no effort to become the behind-the-scenes power that he had been with Wilson. He died in New York City on March 28, 1938.

Born in Virginia in 1827, Alexander W. Terrell was taken to Missouri by his family in 1832. Terrell graduated from the University of Missouri, studied law, and in 1849 was admitted to the bar. In 1852 he moved to Texas and soon donned the robes of a judge, serving on the bench of the Second Judicial District Court from 1857 to 1862. After a brilliant military career in the Confederate army, in which he rose to the rank of brigadier general, and a brief self-imposed exile to Mexico at the close of the fighting, Terrell returned to Houston to practice law. In 1875, by which time he was settled in Austin, he entered politics and was elected to the state senate. He served in the upper house of the legislature until 1882, then later as a representative, for a total of sixteen years' service in the legislature. Judge Terrell was the author of considerable important legislation, including the act that required jurors to be able to read and write, the bill creating the Texas Railroad Commission, the law providing for the exchange of West Texas land for a capitol building, and the Terrell Election Law. During the second administration of President Grover Cleveland, Judge Terrell served as the United States Minister to Turkey. He died in Mineral Wells on September 8, 1912. Terrell County was named in his honor in 1905.

Among the younger Texans entering the national government during this period were several men who gained prominence. Senator Morris Sheppard moved into the Senate in 1913 after a dozen years in the House of Representatives. He introduced and sponsored the measure that became the Eighteenth Amendment to the Constitution, the prohibition amendment, and assisted Andrew J. Volstead in writing the law that enforced alcoholic abstinence.

In 1932 he became chairman of the Military Affairs Committee and was a ranking member of the Commerce Committee at the time of his death in 1941.

Sam T. Rayburn, a native of Tennessee was born in January 1882. After serving several terms in the Texas legislature, including a period as speaker of the House, he was elected to the national House of Representatives in 1912. For almost half a century he held the same seat. Rayburn was speaker of the House of Representatives longer than any other man in history, serving in either that capacity or as majority leader for some forty years. He became one of the most honored of all Texans in Washington and an influential leader in the Democratic party. His funeral in Bonham in 1961 was attended by President John F. Kennedy and former Presidents Harry Truman and Dwight Eisenhower.

Albert Sidney Burleson was best known for his service as postmaster general in the Wilson cabinet. A native of San Marcos, Burleson was educated at the Agricultural and Mechanical College of Texas and the University of Texas. Once district attorney for the Twenty-sixth Judicial District, he was for sixteen years a member of Congress from Austin; he served on the committees of Agriculture, Appropriations, Census, and Foreign Affairs and was the author of much agricultural legislation. Burleson was appointed postmaster general by Wilson in March 1913; during his eight-year tenure, the United States Post Office had a spectacular growth, developing air mail and parcel post service. In 1918 he was named head of the Telegraph and Telephone Administration and two years later led the American Commission to the International Wire Communication Conference. Burleson retired from public life in 1921 and died in November 1937.

Thomas Watt Gregory, born in Mississippi in 1861,

graduated from the Southwestern Presbyterian University of Tennessee in 1883, attended the University of Virginia, and took a law degree at the University of Texas in 1885. He set up his practice in Austin, serving as city attorney from 1891 to 1894. In 1900 he went into a partnership with Robert L. Batts; this firm acted as special counsel for the state in the Waters-Pierce case and other antitrust suits. A delegate to the Democratic national convention in 1904 and 1912, Gregory helped House secure the nomination of Woodrow Wilson. For this service, Gregory was appointed a special assistant to the United States attorney general in 1913 and the next year became attorney general in the Wilson cabinet. In that office Gregory established the War Emergency Division of the Department of Justice, enlarged the Federal Bureau of Investigation, and continued to prosecute the trusts. In 1916 he was offered but declined the office of chief justice of the United States Supreme Court. He left the cabinet in March 1919 when he went to Europe as an advisor at the peace conference. Shortly after his return to the United States, he settled in Houston. He spent his remaining years working for the betterment of the University of Texas, serving eight years on its Board of Regents, and writing several pamphlets. Gregory died in 1933 in New York City, where he had gone to confer with Franklin D. Roosevelt.

David Franklin Houston was the scholar in politics. Born in North Carolina in 1866, he graduated from South Carolina College in 1887 and for the next three years was superintendent of schools at Spartanburg. He then studied for three years at Harvard University, receiving the Master of Arts degree; subsequently he was awarded no less than eight honorary Doctor of Laws degrees. Appointed to the faculty of the University of Texas in 1894, he served as its dean from 1899 to 1902. From 1902 to 1905 he was president of the Agricultural and Mechanical College of Texas, and from 1905 to 1908 he served as the head of the University of Texas. When he accepted the chancellorship of Washington University at St. Louis in 1908, he ended a brilliant fourteen-year academic career in Texas. In 1913 President Wilson persuaded Houston to take the post of secretary of agriculture, and he remained there for seven years during which time several important changes were made. In addition Houston helped organize the Federal Reserve System in 1914 and sat on the Council of National Defense from 1916 to 1920. From February 1920 to March 1921 he was secretary of the treasury and also chairman of the Federal Reserve Board and the Federal Farm Loan Board. After his retirement from governmental service, Houston had an equally distinguished record in the business world. From 1921 to 1930 he was vice-president of the American Telephone and Telegraph Company, and from June 1930 until January 1940 he was president of the Mutual Life Insurance Company. He then served as the chairman of the board of the latter company until his death a few months later. In addition to these positions he was a member of the board of directors of several other large companies and was a trustee of Columbia University. Houston also found time to write several highly respected academic works.

Thus it was that during the opening years of the twentieth century Texans could find as many reasons for pride as for bickering among themselves. They saw their state make sweeping reforms in many fields and their political leaders playing a leading role in the national government. Indeed there had been mighty changes within the span of just a few years, but even greater ones lurked just around the corner.

3

The Era of Farmer Jim

THE VARIOUS GOVERNORS of Texas have used many routes to get to that high office; rangers, generals, farmers, businessmen, lawyers—all have sat in the chief executive's chair. The most frequently traveled road, however, has been up through the hierarchy of local and district offices to the state level, the candidate gradually building a reputation and a following among the voters until his name becomes widely known. Then he seeks the state's top administrative position.

Such was not the case with James Edward Ferguson.

Perhaps no governor of Texas before or since him was known by so few of his fellow citizens when he decided to run for office, for in 1914 Ferguson had never campaigned for an elective position at any level. Certainly very few aspirants to the governorship of Texas have had so varied a background.

Born in 1871 near Salado in Bell County, Ferguson's youth was one of privation and hard work. His father died when Jim was only four years old. His mother remained on the family farm, and there the boy began to work in the fields as soon as he was old enough to help. As a consequence of the family's poverty, young Jim received little formal education. At the age of sixteen he left home for California where he worked in the vineyards, on wheat farms, in placer mines, and at a barbed wire factory. The following year, 1888, he moved first to Nevada, then to Colorado, supporting himself once again in the mines. In Denver he was employed for a time as a bellboy at a local hotel.

After two years of itinerate labor, Ferguson at the age of eighteen returned to Bell County, Texas, where for the next eight years he farmed and labored at occasional odd jobs. Then, following a brief study of law, he was admitted to the bar in 1897 and opened a law office in Belton. In December 1899 he was married to Miriam A. Wallace, daughter of a prominent and successful farmer.

Since his law practice did not fully occupy his time, Ferguson soon expanded his business interests to include real estate, insurance, and finally banking. First connected with the Farmers State Bank of Belton, he moved to Temple in 1907 to help establish the Temple State Bank. Also in Temple he founded a large mercantile firm.

As a leading businessman in his region, he naturally developed an interest in politics. In Bell County he was an active anti-prohibitionist and served as county campaign manager for Congressman Robert L. Henry of Waco in the election of 1902. He supported Cone Johnson's fight against Senator Bailey for delegate-at-large to the Democratic national convention in 1908, was campaign manager for R. V. Davidson in the attorney general's race in 1910, and campaigned for O. B. Colquitt, the successful gubernatorial candidate in 1912. Nevertheless, this experience, while interesting to the citizens of Temple and Bell County, did not give Ferguson a wide acquaintance over the state. Therefore it came as a surprise when he announced in November 1913 that he would be a candidate for the governorship the following year.

According to the rumors current at the time, Ferguson was influenced to enter the race by two factors: his personal feeling that the Texas voters must be tired of the prohibition issue, which along with Baileyism had caused endless debate and division among the citizens of Texas, and his discovery that some fifty-five percent of the state's qualified voters were members of tenant farmer families, a group to whom no candidate had yet made a specific appeal. In his opening speech Ferguson seemed to confirm the rumors. He stated that he would steer clear of both factions in the prohibition issue and that he would campaign on more vital topics. In an effort to end entirely the prohibition question, he declared that if elected he would veto all liquor legislation that might be brought before him. He then proposed the passage of a law fixing the rental of tenant farms at not more than one third of the grain and one fourth of the cotton produced (the tenant furnishing the teams and tools), making any higher rate illegal, and eliminating the growing practice of requiring from the tenant a bonus for the rental of the better farms.

Ferguson also advocated better educational facilities, especially in the public schools; penitentiary reform; a system of state-controlled bonded warehouses for the storage of surplus crops; and the building of improved highways. He declared that the movement to decrease railroad rates was wrong, that the railroads were entitled to make a profit; however, he said he believed in the regulation of the roads to make them safer and to insure reasonable service to the people.

The tenant farmer plank in the Ferguson platform, an entirely new issue in Texas politics, attracted attention to the candidate, and throughout his campaign his speeches were heard invariably by audiences containing a majority of tenant farmers and their friends. That the Ferguson plan to regulate the amount that could be charged for renting farms drew widespread attention is illustrated by the fact that the faraway London *Times* devoted almost a full page in a Sunday issue to a discussion and analysis of his proposal and chances of success in the election.

"Farmer Jim," as he became known during the campaign, had miscalculated, however, when he decided that the voters were tired of the prohibition issue. They were not. The prohibitionists in the Democratic party held a convention before the primary and pledged their support to Thomas H. Ball of Houston, a former congressman who had been chairman of the prohibition campaign committee in the statewide contest in 1911. The anti-prohibitionists held a similar convention, but Ferguson refused to attend or to seek their support, stating that he would have nothing to do with either faction in the wet-dry struggle. The convention adjourned without endorsing Ferguson, but its members went home determined to support him and other anti-prohibitionists withdrew from the primary. Ferguson therefore went to the polls against Ball as the candidate of the wets. They supported him because of his pledge that should he become governor he would veto all liquor legislation. That pledge to the wets meant a promise to maintain the *status quo,* and Texas had voted wet in recent elections.

The campaign that followed was one of the most colorful in Texas history. Early in the campaign Colonel Ball began to insist that the leading question of the election was whether or not the liquor interests should dominate the politics and government of Texas. Ball argued that it was ridiculous to say that prohibition was not an issue in the campaign; Ferguson, he said, stood for the open saloon. His proof for his statement was the fact that Governor Colquitt, an anti-prohibitionist, was campaigning for Ferguson.

Ball was an enthusiastic supporter of the Woodrow Wilson policies on the national level, and in turn he received support from Washington leaders. Also, since the prohibition cause was identified with the progressive element in the Democratic party, many state and national leaders announced their support of Ball because of his dry stand. Cone Johnson, solicitor in the Department of State in the Wilson administration, urged Texans to vote for Ball. Colonels John N. Simpson of Dallas and R. M. Johnson, editor of the Houston *Post,* announced for Ball as did John H. Ṣtephens of Denton, who said he had served with Ball in Congress for six years and had found him a patriotic servant of the people and worthy of any honor. Among the prominent speakers for Ball were M. M. Crane, Thomas M. Campbell, and Senator Morris Sheppard. Even Joe Bailey came out for Ball, saying the Ferguson tenant plank was socialistic. National leaders who urged the election of Ball included President Woodrow Wilson, Secretary of State William Jennings Bryan, Postmaster General Albert Burleson, and Secretary of Agriculture David F. Houston. Ferguson retaliated by severely criticizing the federal officials, saying they had disregarded the principles of states' rights and the doctrine of local self-government.

Both candidates carried their campaigns to all parts of the state. Ferguson continued his appeals to the farmers and small businessmen, insisting that prohibition was not an issue. Ball appealed to the progressives and the Wilson admirers, said that Ferguson was out of line with the national administration, and repeated often that his opponent advocated control of Texas by the liquor interests.

Tempers grew more than usually heated as the warm days of July appeared and the Democratic primary neared. "The People's Candidate," Ferguson's admirers called him. "The Peanut Candidate," sneered the drys in reply. Ball's supporters referred to their candidate's dry "heart of oak plank." The anti-prohibitionists, in their support of Ferguson, called for votes from "all who would not like to have their liquid freedom cut off."

Finally the editor of the Bryan *Daily Eagle* had enough of the tension of the race. "Now is the time," he wrote, "that the candidates should visit the farmers, each candidate spending at least half a day with each farmer and putting in the time not in talk, but in chopping cotton. The best choppers would no doubt be in public favor, at least as long as cotton chopping held out."

Election day eventually arrived, and with it came a startling upset. The vote was 237,062 for Ferguson; 191,558 for Ball. A complete political unknown had won the highest office in the state in opposition to the combined forces of the state's leading politicians and the President of the United States. And in doing so, he carried not only his home county of Bell by 860 votes, but Ball's home county of Harris as well by a margin of 3,399 (8,777 to 5,378).

Ferguson as governor proved as good as his word. Immediately after his inauguration, he reminded the Thirty-fourth Legislature that Texans were poor, that the price of cotton was low, that Europe was at war, and therefore that the new budget should not be extravagant. In one paragraph of his message to the legislature he explained in detail what should be done to safeguard tenant farmers against ruinous contracts with their landlords. He recommended laws to protect child laborers and to prohibit pools, combinations, and trusts "formed for the purpose of fixing the price of the product of the farm"; he asked for legislation designed to attract investors to Texas, to provide liberally for all institutions of higher learning, to make generous appropriations for the improvement of rural schools, to build new highways with convict labor, to reform the judiciary, to exempt cotton and woolen factories from taxation in order to attract such industries to the state, to protect the livestock producers, and to bring together the landless man and the homeless land.

The legislature responded to Ferguson's message in a relatively harmonious session with much constructive legislation. A farm tenant bill limiting rent on Texas farms as suggested by Ferguson was accepted in the Senate by a vote of 23 to 4 and in the House by 100 to 24; but the act was not rigidly enforced and was declared unconstitutional in 1921. A law to make school attendance compulsory and another to establish rural high schools were enacted. Also passed was a rural school aid bill specifying that in order to qualify the rural school district should first levy a local school tax of not less than fifty cents on the hundred dollars of valuation of property. This law resulted in greatly increased support of schools in areas where help was most needed, and the administration gained many friends through the policy. Also, later legislatures continued the practice of appropriating increasing amounts for rural school aid, with the result that innumerable rural school children have received a much better education than those of the pre-Ferguson era.

Governor Ferguson worked closely with the legislature and thereby won many new supporters because of his farm and school policies. He expected to win reelection in 1916 by a comfortable majority, but nevertheless considered it expedient to campaign. His opponent in the race was Charles H. Morris, a wealthy banker who had lived in several East Texas towns, including Hughes Springs, Pittsburg, and Winnsboro. Morris was a leader in the Methodist church and a lifelong prohibitionist. He had first appeared on the political scene in 1914 when he announced for governor on a progressive platform; he favored the repeal of the poll tax prerequisite for voting, the establishment of a one-house legislature, a pension for mothers, compulsory school attendance, free textbooks, and better salaries for teachers. Morris made no real campaign in 1914 and received fewer than seven thousand votes as a result. But in 1916 he came out fighting, basing his campaign on presumed weaknesses of the first Ferguson administration, its extravagances, and the alleged mismanagement and misappropriation of public funds by the governor. Morris in 1916 favored lower taxes, reduction of office expenses, better schools, and a businesslike administration for the state.

During the 1916 campaign Morris charged that Ferguson had used for personal expenses state funds appropriated for law enforcement, the capture of criminals, and other purposes. At many of his rallies, Morris exhibited lists of grocery bills of the executive mansion—paid, he claimed, with state money by Ferguson. The total of state funds used by Ferguson for personal expenses amounted, said Morris, to more than two thousand dollars. He charged that "Farmer Jim" had sold out the farmers and ginners in the warehouse law that had been passed, that the governor had exaggerated the school expense figures in the increase over the last biennium, and that Ferguson had misrepresented the facts in explaining why higher taxes had been levied. On the positive side, Morris advocated a plan whereby tenant farmers could become home owners through long-term, low-interest state loans.

In his six-week campaign for reelection, Ferguson said that peace and harmony had existed between himself and the legislature and defended his administration against charges of extravagance. He tried to justify his use of unauthorized funds for the mansion grocery bills, saying that he would do the same thing again if he had his term to live over.

The voting public seemed inclined to believe Ferguson, and political experts across the state were predicting the reelection of the incumbent. For the most part the voters seemed to consider Morris's charges against the governor to be no more than the usual "mudslinging" present in every campaign.

Then during the last few weeks before the primary election Morris brought forward two new and startling charges. He declared that Ferguson's 1914 campaign had been financed by a Houston brewery to the amount of thirty thousand dollars. In that allegation, which raised all the emotional heat and fury of the wet-dry struggle, he was supported by C. E. Maedgen, then vice-president of the Temple State Bank. The second charge was even stronger than the first; Morris said that Ferguson had collected the insurance, amounting to $100,000, on West Texas State

Normal College at Canyon, destroyed by fire, and had put the money in his bank at Temple, refusing to pay the state any interest on that sum.

Ferguson immediately denied both charges. He stated that no brewing companies had supported his candidacy in 1914 and that he had not used for his own advantage the Canyon normal school insurance money. He was supported by other officials of the Temple State Bank in his story.

Following the Morris and Maedgen charges, the usual formidable group of veteran prohibition leaders made speeches for Morris and denounced Ferguson. But the public sided with Ferguson, and he was reelected. His vote was 240,561, slightly more than in 1914 (237,062); the vote for Morris was only 174,611, almost twenty thousand fewer than Ball had received.

Actually the voting public in 1916 was far more interested in the senatorial race than in the one for governor. Ex-Governor Colquitt was leading the professional wets in an attempt to unseat the prohibitionist Culberson. A veritable crusade among the drys sent a host of patriotic speakers over the state for Culberson, who was in failing health and could not come to Texas for the campaign or leave his work as a war leader in the Senate. The result was a resounding victory for Culberson and the drys— 155,410 to 88,435.

The year 1916 saw the "usual" campaign for submission of the question of prohibition to the voters. A "straw vote" was taken at the same time as the primary on whether or not the people wished the legislature to submit a prohibition amendment at the next general election; submission carried by only two thousand votes, and the issue was ignored by the Ferguson legislature.

Governor Ferguson went into his second term with increased prestige. His address to the Thirty-fifth Legislature was one of the shortest ever made by a governor to that body as it convened; he asked for special attention to the needs of the farmers and day laborers of the state, aid of a million dollars a year for rural schools, itemization of all appropriations, authorization of a state highway commission, an absentee voting law, congressional redistricting, and a new insane asylum. To aid law enforcement and the courts in the state, he called for legislation to provide for judicial reform to relieve the overburdened Supreme Court, a stronger Ranger force, and a prohibition on carrying guns. The governor pleaded with the legislators, saying, "The people need us both to accomplish those things which represent their will."

And again the session was relatively harmonious, with the governor getting many of the things he had requested. A highway commission was established with the power to oversee the spending of federal aid funds for road improvement, and a road building program was planned. Speed limits for automobile driving in the state were set at eighteen miles an hour in rural areas, fifteen miles an hour in cities. Automobiles were required to come to a stop at least seventy-five feet away from railroad crossings. New laws were passed to aid the Supreme Court, and judges were voted higher salaries. Public school aid of a million dollars a year was approved, just as the governor had requested.

The Thirty-fifth Legislature had a mind of its own, however, and did some things the governor did not want. For example, it voted to submit to the electorate the question of calling a convention to rewrite the Constitution of 1876. After a spirited controversy, Ferguson vetoed the referendum, saying that fundamental changes in the state's government should not be considered while the country was at war and many of the men were not at home to vote.

Following adjournment of the legislature, William M. Thornton of the Dallas *News* best reflected the public reaction when he reviewed with both praise and condemnation the work of the session. He began by saying that it was "certainly a pork-barrel legislature." If there were no vetoes, he said, the state would have one new agricultural and mechanical college, three or four junior agricultural colleges, "and normal schools too numerous to mention." The editor urged the governor to veto the new schools, charging that all of them had passed the legislature through log-rolling tactics. Worthy of praise, Thornton declared, were the liberal provisions for public schools, judicial reform, legislation for good roads, and measures for the eradication of ticks.

What Thornton failed to mention as either good or bad was the $1,600,000 appropriation for the University of Texas; however, it was this item that led to the hottest political struggle ever seen in the state to that time. Shortly after the legislature adjourned, Governor Ferguson announced that he was line vetoing practically the entire University appropriation. He did so because the board of regents of that institution had failed to remove several faculty members whom the governor found objectionable and because the board refused to carry out his suggestion to abolish fraternities and sororities.

The reaction to the governor's veto was immediate and widespread. Public excitement ran wild as ex-students, faculty, and friends raised a cry for academic freedom. Making a loud clamor, they rushed to do battle with Ferguson to get the appropriation restored.

The "University Crowd" was joined by the host of Ferguson enemies, and soon the charges that had been made against the governor during the gubernatorial campaign of 1916 were renewed and additional charges levelled. In connection with those charges a Travis County grand jury summoned Ferguson to appear on July 21, 1917, and a few days later indicted him on nine counts. Seven of the nine were related to the misapplication of public funds, one to embezzlement, and one to the diversion of a special fund to his own use. The governor calmly made bond of $13,000 and announced his candidacy for a third term.

The speaker of the House of Representatives on July 23 issued a call for a special session of that body "for the purpose of considering the impeachment of the governor." There was some doubt about the legality of the speaker's call, and many of the experts, including prominent and experienced lawyers over the state, voiced opinions in the newspapers. Ferguson insisted that only the governor could call the legislature or a part of it into special session, but even his attorney general, a personal and political friend, stated that for the purpose of impeaching the governor the speaker had the legal right to issue the call. The pressure mounted.

Just three days before the date set by the speaker for the legislature to convene, Ferguson—hard pressed by both enemies and friends—said he would "just make it legal" and issued a call for both houses to meet for the purpose of making appropriations for the University.

The House of Representatives did make the necessary appropriation, but that bill occupied very little of its time. The legislators were more interested in the solemn drama of impeachment, the real reason why they had been called to Austin. After some investigation of the several charges brought against the governor, the House voted twenty-one articles of impeachment. On September 24, 1917, after sitting for three weeks as a High Court of Impeachment, the Senate convicted Ferguson on ten of the charges. Five of the ten dealt with the misapplication of public funds; three concerned his disagreements with the University; one declared that he had failed to respect and enforce the banking laws of the state; and one charged that during the 1916 campaign he had accepted $156,500 in currency from a source or sources he refused to reveal. Nine of the accusations were for violations of the law; the tenth—receipt of $156,500 from a secret source—was not strictly illegal, but it could not be defended as a good policy. The Court of Impeachment, by a vote of 25 to 3, removed Ferguson from office and made him ineligible to hold any office of honor, trust, or profit under the State of Texas. In a desperate effort to avoid the restriction on holding office, Ferguson resigned as governor the day before the judgment was announced and insisted that it therefore could not apply to him. The question was finally brought before the courts, and the decision of the Court of Impeachment was sustained.

Ferguson supporters charged that no impeached politician in American history had ever been stripped of his right to hold public office thereafter as had Ferguson. They declared that Ferguson had been so penalized because his enemies feared the people of Texas would re-elect him to some position of trust and thus vindicate him of the charges that had been made and voted upon.

But if James Ferguson's political rights had been stripped from him, his voice and his influence had not. And Ferguson intended that both should be felt. Immediately after he was removed, he took his family back to Temple where he founded the *Ferguson Forum,* a small newspaper which he used as a mighty club against his enemies. The prohibitionists dubbed the paper "The Ferguson For Rum," charging that it was merely a device for getting campaign funds from breweries (they said that a one-page advertisement in the *Forum* cost $100,-000). In every Texas election between 1918 and 1936, a Ferguson-backed candidate was in one of the major election races in Texas, and biennially the former governor took to the campaign trail to harangue the Texas voters.

If Ferguson's enemies had hoped to remove him from the political scene by the prohibition against his holding public office, they certainly had failed.

4

William P. Hobby
and the War

"Do your bit!" screamed war posters from every corner and telephone pole in Austin, just as elsewhere in the nation, in August 1917, and everywhere patriotic Americans were striving to do their fair share. But for one man in Austin on August 24, a "bit" would not be good enough. William Pettus Hobby, the lieutenant governor of Texas, was facing a crisis even hotter than the summer weather; he had come face to face with destiny.

The afternoon before, the House of Representatives of the state legislature had voted twenty-one articles of impeachment against James Ferguson. Constitutionally, the governor was thereby automatically suspended until he was either cleared or convicted of the charges, the lieutenant governor carrying out the duties of the office in the interim.

At ten o'clock on the morning of August 24, Hobby walked into Ferguson's office for the transfer of authority. The governor was cordial, and the business was quickly done. Then Hobby, in an effort to ease the awkward situation, suggested that Ferguson continue to occupy the governor's mansion and the executive suite in the capitol. Both offers were accepted, and for the next month acting Governor Hobby lived at the Driskill Hotel in Austin and conducted the chief executive's functions from the lieutenant governor's office.

As acting governor, Hobby immediately found himself confronted with a multitude of problems, each demanding swift, positive attention: emergency action was needed in order that Texas might do its part toward winning the war; fear, almost amounting to hysteria, gripped some of the people along the coast and in South Texas owing to rumors about German submarines operating near Galveston and because of reported German intrigues in northern Mexico; the state was suffering from a terrible and prolonged drouth; pink bollworms were threatening the life of the Texas cotton industry; and the wet-dry struggle was approaching a bitter climax. Amidst these difficulties, Hobby found that he could not count on help from the many Ferguson appointees and friends in the administration. They naturally resented anyone who succeeded Ferguson as chief executive of the state.

Will Hobby was not a man to be envied that August morning when he became acting governor, but he was one who had come a long way in life.

He was born in Moscow, Polk County, Texas, in 1878. There he lived until the age of fourteen when his father, the district judge, failed to win reelection. The Hobby family thereupon moved to Houston where young Will was enrolled in the public high school. In that city he grew to manhood. In stature he was short, and he had embarrassingly large ears. In the bitter election of 1918 Jim Ferguson attempted to ridicule Hobby by describing him as "a misfit whom God had failed to endow with the physical attributes that make up a man." Hobby's answer left no doubts that his mental capacity or his political astuteness were as big as anyone's, perhaps greater than most: "I will admit that the Supreme Being failed to favor me with physical attributes pleasing to Governor Ferguson, but at least He gave me the intelligence to know the difference between my own money and that which belongs to the state."

Next door to the Houston high school was the office and plant of the Houston *Post*, and nearly every day after classes were over, Will stopped by to talk with the reporters and to absorb the atmosphere of the newspaper world. He had discovered his life's occupation. At the age of sixteen he quit school and went to work as a clerk in the circulation department of the *Post*. He rose rapidly, becoming a reporter in 1901 and just two years later the youngest managing editor in the history of that newspaper.

The Panic of 1907 brought financial distress to the Beaumont *Enterprise*, and local businessmen persuaded Hobby to move to their city to become the editor and publisher of the paper. He used five thousand dollars which he borrowed to become half owner of the *Enterprise*, moved to Beaumont, and soon had the paper on a sound basis. As a businessman, a civic organizer, and a leader in the successful drive to get a deepwater channel linking Beaumont with the Gulf of Mexico, Hobby gained prominence and recognition, both locally and across the state.

The *Enterprise* invariably supported candidates of the Democratic party and Hobby had worked hard in several elections, but in 1914 he had never run for office himself. That year, however, his friends urged him to enter the race for lieutenant governor. After lengthy consideration he consented, and as a staunch foe of prohibition he won the office by a narrow margin. Two years later he had no opponent in his bid for reelection and was returned to the lieutenant governor's office for another term. Thus it was that in 1917 he was called upon to become acting governor, almost the youngest chief executive in the state's history.

During the subsequent trial in the High Court of Impeachment, Hobby avoided the limelight as much as possible. The only matters he took up were those of utmost urgency. The Thirty-fifth Legislature was already in its second called session when he took office; the first had passed the general appropriation bill, enacted a free textbook law, created a State Council of Defense, and authorized certain independent school districts. The second called session dealt primarily with the trial and impeachment of the governor, but it did pass and on August 31 send to Hobby for his signature an appropriation for the University.

On that last day of August the third special session, called by acting Governor Hobby, began. It continued the trial of Ferguson and finally ousted him. On September 22 ten of the articles of impeachment were upheld; three days later Ferguson was removed. Before the senators could put the finishing touches on the act and make it official, Ferguson went to the secretary of state's office and turned in his resignation in an effort to avoid the penalty clause forbidding him ever again to hold a public office in the state. By one or the other of these two acts (that of the governor or that of the Senate), William P. Hobby became governor of the state.

The third special session of the legislature also dealt with other matters as specified by Hobby: drouth relief, protection of servicemen from civil suits, and the problem of the pink bollworms. Everything asked by Hobby was done.

A mild-mannered and quiet man personally, the new governor performed his duties during the fall of 1917 with becoming modesty. In a speech at Tyler he praised the war policies of President Wilson, appealed to all Texans to make even greater sacrifices for their country, and pledged himself to work for a reduction in state expenses. A week later he opened the Texas State Fair at Dallas with a speech repeating the pledges made at Tyler. He worked closely with the State Council of Defense, he journeyed to Washington in connection with drouth relief, and he called on the Special House Investigating Committee to audit all state departments, visit all state institutions, particularly the prisons, inquire into every department with an appointive head, and make recommendations for saving money.

Early in February 1918 he called the fourth special session of the Thirty-fifth Legislature to consider a host of needed reforms. The representatives of the people responded by passing ninety-five general laws, including ratification of the Eighteenth Amendment to the United States Constitution (prohibition). Bootlegging was made a felony, two million dollars was appropriated for the purchasing of feed and seed in drouth-stricken counties, women were given the right to vote in party primary elections, and an attempt was made to improve moral conditions near military posts in the state.

Hobby and the legislators were proud of the accomplishments of the February-March 1918 special session, but they found that most of their activities and laws had been crowded off the front pages of the newspapers by stories about the war and the patriotic efforts of the people at home. During the first fourteen months of the Hobby administration, the war was foremost in the minds of the people.

Texas has always enthusiastically supported the wars of the United States, and the conflict of 1917-1918 was no exception. In Washington, numerous Texans served in the Wilson cabinet or on the various war boards and agencies; Texans in Congress played a leading role in securing the passage of war legislation desired by the President. Still other Texans were equally prominent as military leaders, and 197,389 young men from the Lone Star State either volunteered or were drafted. With flags waving, bands playing, and the cheers of their fellow citizens ringing in their ears, these men marched off to war, serving primarily in Texas commands such as the Thirty-sixth and Ninetieth divisions; several Texas companies, in addition, were in the Forty-second Division. Men were not the only ones to serve in uniform during the war; some 450 Texas women went along as members of the Nurses Corps.

Texas cooperated fully with the national draft laws. The state's selective service organization, directed by Major John C. Townes, supervised a hierarchy of sub-agencies that reached into every town and rural community. Under the first national draft registration act nearly four hundred thousand Texans between the ages of twenty-one and thirty were registered for possible military duty; the second act, which extended the age limit both upward and downward, brought the total to 988,068.

When the fighting was concluded in Europe and the men started returning—marching to the tune of "When Johnny Comes Marching Home Again" or "Over There"— more than five thousand Texans had been killed and buried abroad.

Because of its mild climate and relative dryness, Texas was the location of a large number of training camps. Thousands of young Americans received their first glimpse of the Lone Star State as members of the armed forces during World War I. The number of bases in the state can easily be seen from the fact that in February 1918 when the legislature was considering a law (subsequently passed) barring the sale of alcoholic beverages within ten miles of a military post, those opposing the measure protested that such legislation would make almost ninety percent of Texas dry.

Camp Travis at San Antonio was the nation's largest training camp during the war; other Texas camps included Camp Bowie at Fort Worth, Camp MacArthur at Waco, and Camp Logan at Houston. Other posts, established years earlier—such as Fort Sam Houston at San Antonio and Fort Bliss at El Paso—rendered invaluable service, as did the officer training school at Leon Springs (near San Antonio).

Perhaps most startling of all to Texans, however, were the flight training bases established in the state, providing for many their first glimpse of an airplane. Kelly Field at San Antonio was opened in July 1917 as a primary training center for pilots and mechanics. The hastily constructed field was hardly a reassuring sight to the cadets circling overhead; one of them described it as "a vast triangular area of brown Bermuda grass bordered by a mesquite 'fault' on one side, a white ribbon of highway on the other and . . . a base composed of a hangar line supported by a maze of squat, one-story frame buildings interlaced with gray streets and roads." Two other air bases at San Antonio—Brooks Field, which trained instructors and aerial observers, and Wise Field, which was operated by the army balloon school—made it a nationally outstanding aviation city.

In addition to the complex at San Antonio, there were air bases at five other Texas cities: Ellington Field near Houston, where bombing, gunnery, aerial photography, and navigation were taught; Taliaferro Field at Fort Worth, where a three weeks' course in aerial gunnery was conducted; Love Field and Camp Dick in Dallas, where aspiring pilots were taught; Rich Field at Waco, which specialized in primary flight instruction; and Call Field at Wichita Falls, where aerial observers were trained.

Ninety-five percent of the pilots trained in Texas received their instruction in the Curtis Standard JN4D Military Tractor, a ninety-horsepower biplane that was surprisingly reliable. Cadets were given six to eight weeks of primary training, four weeks of advanced instruction, and then were sent to Europe. Combat tactics they had to learn on the job. Casualties at the training fields were high primarily because students were not taught how to recover from spins. Unfortunately, most instructors had no idea what caused an airplane to go into one, nor did they know how to recover control when a spin developed.

Only a small percentage of the Texas population marched or flew off to war; the majority stayed home and tried to do their part there. They were well organized in their patriotic efforts by the State Council of Defense, a branch of the National Council of Defense. Under the chairmanship of O. E. Dunlap of Waxahachie, the state

World War I Aviation

council tried to coordinate the efforts of the state with those of the nation. Helping in the task were 240 county and 15,000 community councils. Their work consisted of selling Liberty Bonds, securing support for the Red Cross, promoting recreational facilities for soldiers in the state, and attempting to find ways to improve the troops' morale. And the councils, both at the local and state level, tried to publicize and popularize the war effort: they distributed pamphlets, promoted the conservation of food, and kept a watch for disloyal words or deeds. When the war was over at last, the council helped the returning veterans find employment.

Herbert Hoover, the national food administrator, popularized the slogan, "Food Will Win the War," and Texans, along with the rest of the country, were asked to do their part. Directed by E. A. Peden of Houston, the food administration's Texas branch conducted a campaign in the fall of 1917 to get housewives voluntarily to sign pledges to conserve flour, sugar, fats, and meat, but the effort met with only limited success. Thereupon, Peden and his workers shifted their campaign to the merchants, requesting them to conform to definite rules to insure both fair distribution and conservation. A "wheat fast" was imposed on the state for two months in 1918; it provided that no wheat would be shipped into Texas and that wheat grown in the state would be sent to the allies.

The period of the war was one of steadily rising food prices and generally mild inflation. Along with the rise in family expenses came an increase in state and public expenditures which continued at the higher rate after the war was over. Between 1913 and 1919 the total annual budget for the state increased from thirteen million dollars per year to twenty-seven million dollars.

As late as November 9, 1918, Governor Hobby was

still promoting the war effort. He designated that day as a time for Texans to gather materials for gas masks. The following day, although ill with flu, he attended a memorial service for men from Austin who had been killed in the war. Then at three o'clock on the morning of November 11, Texans were awakened by the firing of shotguns, the honking of automobile horns, the blasts of factory whistles, and the cries of excited citizens. An armistice had been signed, and the war was over!

Almost unnoticed in the excitement was the outcome of the general election that had been held only a few days earlier. No one was paying much attention anyway, for Texas elections had always been decided in the Democratic primary in July. In addition, Texans had almost exhausted the year's quota of political enthusiasm during the primary and had little left for the general election; the Democratic primary in 1918 was one of the most colorful spectacles in the state's history, pitting Will Hobby against Jim Ferguson. Hobby was campaigning for the traditional second term to which most governors feel they are entitled; Ferguson was fighting for "vindication," a cause in which he thoroughly believed.

Ferguson had announced his candidacy for a third term at the time he was removed from office. Inasmuch as the State Democratic Executive Committee had been chosen at the preceding state convention, which Ferguson had dominated, its members accepted his application and placed his name on the Democratic primary ballot despite the ban on his holding public office. In the spring of 1918 Ferguson supporters, including lawyers and judges, wrote letters published in the newspapers, declaring that Ferguson's impeachment was void (because he had resigned before his removal) and that there was thus no bar to his holding office if elected. They also claimed that the prohibition Democrats had planned all along to get rid of Ferguson and had used the "University muddle" as an excuse. They declared that a great wrong had been done the former governor, and that the only way the people could undo the injustice was to reelect him.

Ex-Governor Ferguson opened his campaign in April, contending that all his troubles had come from trying to provide educational facilities for the poor people. He answered his critics as only he could, ridiculing the research work at the University of Texas. Derisively he told of one University professor who had spent two years in an attempt to grow wool on the back of an armadillo. He called the faculty "butterfly chasers," "day dreamers," "educated fools," "liars," and "two-bit thieves." He charged the administration with "vicious extravagances" and predicted that some day other nations would be raising armies to put down the University "autocracy" unless the people put their heels on it very quickly. He declared that on the University payroll were the names of dead men, that the school's administration was made up of crooks and grafters, and that the chief issue of the campaign was whether or not the University would rule the state.

Ferguson demonstrated again and again during the spring of 1918 that he had not lost his ability as a campaigner and that he knew the way to appeal to the voters of Texas. When a friend in Austin wrote that Governor Hobby was building a tennis court behind the executive mansion, Ferguson wrote a long article in the *Forum,* concluding that he personally preferred a pen for milk cows to a sissified place for holding games as did the "political accident," Hobby.

Answering the charge, Hobby declared, "It's too bad that the ex-Governor didn't think of the . . . cow pen while he was in office. They say that in those days he confined his milking activities to the public treasury." Nevertheless, work was stopped on the tennis court, and a flock of chickens was installed instead.

Governor Hobby conducted his campaign on a platform stressing his accomplishments while in office and promising more assistance for education, good roads, and tenant farmers who wished to acquire their own land. He promised to recommend an appropriation of one million dollars for aid to weak county schools. He declared that his administration had done much to "get the farmer out of the mud," and that he would continue to work for more and better roads. He pulled no punches in the contest, and he and his supporters revived and repeated all the old charges against Ferguson. They built a strong case against the impeached governor, pointing to his early opposition to the Wilson war measures, his opposition to woman suffrage, his finances, and his thoughtless remarks about the patriotism of German-Americans in Texas.

The ex-governor had publicly stated his opposition to the selective service draft law when it first passed in Congress (he soon retracted his objections); the Hobby faction charged him with failure to cooperate with the Wilson administration. "I have not made speeches against the draft law as has the man who claims he is running against me for governor," declared Hobby, who reminded women that he had supported the plan that allowed them to vote in primaries. He and his friends often quoted Ferguson's answer to the suffragettes in 1916: "Women's place is in the home."

Hobby speakers asked their audiences if they wanted a governor who would spend the state's money for his private use, as had Ferguson. Speaking at Temple, Governor Hobby argued that the citizens of Texas were called upon in the election to decide whether they wanted a chief executive who violated the laws by paying off a private debt with state funds or a chief executive who was honest. Again and again, Hobby reminded the voters that his opponent had accepted $156,500 from sources which he refused to divulge.

Maliciously, some Hobby supporters started a whisper campaign that the $156,500 had been given to Ferguson by the German kaiser in return for opposition to the war effort. Hobby, speaking at Crockett, stated that if the ex-governor had not received the money from the ruler of Germany, he had done a great deal of work for him for nothing. Ferguson was not a man who usually worked without fees, concluded Hobby. (The charge, of course, was entirely unfounded. Two Texas brewers, L. A. Adoue of Galveston and Otto Wahrmund of San Antonio, declared that the breweries of Texas had loaned Ferguson the money "when he was in trouble and needed [it]. . . . " They testified that the funds were extended the governor because of his campaign promises that there would be no changes in the prohibition status in Texas. But their testimony was not published until almost a week after the election was over, too late to help Ferguson.)

One of the biggest salvos in the barrage against the former governor was thoughtlessly fired by Ferguson himself. During the campaign Ferguson critized Hobby for appointing Jake Wolters, a "full-blooded German," to the rank of brigadier general in the state militia and for being introduced to South Texas audiences by Senator F. C. Weinert, another "full-blooded German." Both Wolters and Weinert were members of highly respected Texas families that were noted for their patriotism and their honor. The Ferguson remarks doubtlessly were remembered by the large German element in Texas at election time.

Election returns in the July primary showed that Hobby had carried 234 counties and received 461,479 votes; Ferguson carried 20 counties and received 217,012 votes. The mild-mannered newspaperman, Hobby, had polled almost seventy percent of the state's total vote!

The outcome of the general election in November, as usual, was a foregone conclusion. Hobby easily won over his Republican opponent. Noteworthy was the ratification of the amendment to the constitution providing free textbooks for Texas school children. Hobby, who had worked extremely hard to sell the amendment to the voters, was gratified by the returns.

When the Thirty-sixth Legislature convened in January 1919, the governor reminded it that the state had entered a new age, the postwar years, and dwelt upon the fact that Texas had played a large part in winning the war. He then turned to his favorite subject: "Education should claim your first thought. If Texas should have to go broke, let it be for the sake of education. . . ." He urged the appropriation of a half million dollars to supplement the available school fund for the purpose of increasing salaries of public school teachers and said another million dollars should be set aside for schools with enrollments of less than three hundred each. He argued that the state should lend money to heads of families for the purpose of purchasing homes; he favored revising the jurisdiction of the higher courts, calling a constitutional convention to rewrite the state's basic law, and creating a state board of equalization; in addition, he asked for a tax on oil and oil products, natural gas, electric lights, and other industries.

In a relatively harmonious regular session, followed by four called ones, the legislature gave Hobby's program a cordial response. His school proposals were enacted, a tax on oil production was levied, and a state board of control (a central purchasing agency) was authorized. Constitutional amendments, passed for submission to the voters, included a scheme for home loans, statewide prohibition, and the calling of a new constitutional convention. Also readied for the voters' consideration was a woman suffrage amendment, despite the fact that the legislature voted for the Nineteenth Amendment to the United States Constitution (woman suffrage).

The prohibition and woman suffrage referenda were set for May 24, 1919. No spirited or general campaign was conducted for either proposition despite the heated tempers and fights that both issues had precipitated over the years. Prohibition carried by a vote of 158,982 to 130,907, while the suffrage amendment failed by about the same proportion. Nevertheless the suffragettes gained their goal, for the Nineteenth Amendment was ratified and went into effect in the summer of 1920. In the fall of 1919 the amendment calling for a new constitutional convention failed to gain the approval of Texas voters. The amendment to provide home ownership loans, although endorsed by the Democratic state convention, likewise failed.

In January 1921 when he once again became a private citizen, Will Hobby could look back on the three and one-half years with pride. Much had been accomplished. Whatever the criticisms of his administration, it could not be called a "do-nothing" one. Hobby went back to his Beaumont *Enterprise* and in 1922 rejoined the Houston *Post*. Never again did he enter politics, but his wife, the former Oveta Culp, later served in the Eisenhower cabinet.

5

The Years of
Hatred and Fear

"ONCE LEAD THIS PEOPLE INTO WAR," said Woodrow Wilson just before recommending that Congress declare war on Germany, "and they'll forget there ever was such a thing as tolerance. To fight you must be brutal and ruthless, and the spirit of ruthless brutality will enter into every fiber of our national life. . . ."

Unfortunately he was correct.

In Brenham and Washington County, Texas, a membership drive for the American Red Cross was moving slowly in December 1917. A mass meeting was held in the local opera house and a fund was raised by the wealthier citizens to purchase memberships for those unable to pay the fees; for use on those who had money but refused to join, the same meeting voted to purchase an "armload of buggywhips." Shortly after this patriotic meeting adjourned, it was reported that one resident of the community had refused to become a member, commenting, "To Hell with the Red Cross." The next day a number of "influential and esteemed" citizens of Brenham caught the man, along with five like-minded non-joiners. Unmasked and in broad daylight, the good citizens of Brenham gave the six dissenters "a touch of the hot time they wished for the noble international organization." After the flogging, the six men decided to join. The end of the drive found Washington County exceeding its quota by one thousand members.

Not only did such violations of individual rights occur openly, but the newspapers and the public praised it. "The people must act as they did at Brenham," the editor of the Bryan *Daily Eagle* urged his readers. "Whipping may convert some, while others are beyond conversion and should be shot."

Almost every day the newspapers carried stories of sabotage or rumors of it. For example, on May 19, 1917, it was reported that between twenty and forty persons had been arrested at Snyder and charged with a conspiracy against the federal government. The story concluded with the statement that a strong guard had been placed around the town because of a plot to burn it. On July 12 the headlines read, "An Attempt Made To Blow Up the Causeway Across Galveston Bay."

Almost as a matter of course, it was widely assumed that the German-Americans were behind such plots, and everywhere persecution of this group reached fever pitch. "America for Americans" and "100% Americanism" became popular slogans. The legislature responded to the public pressure by passing in the 1918 special session measures prohibiting disloyal language or conduct, providing stiff prison sentences for anyone criticizing the United States, the government, the flag, the uniforms of military personnel, public officials, or our entrance into the war. Another act held that instruction in the public schools had to be conducted in English, that schools had to be equipped with flags and flag poles, and that teachers had to spend at least ten minutes every day teaching patriotism. One legislative committee recommended, and many school boards followed it, that all books of recent date extolling the greatness of Germany be destroyed or boxed and locked away.

The feeling against Germany was carried to such extremes that frankfurters became known as "liberty pups," and sauerkraut was referred to as "liberty cabbage."

That such a spirit of intolerance and superpatriotism did not die away at the end of the war may be seen from the fact that in 1919 Governor Hobby vetoed the appropriation for the German department at the University of Texas, declaring that the elimination of the courses that department offered would bring about purer Americanism. In 1918 the legislature had provided that only citizens of the United States could vote. And in 1923 a law requiring the teaching of the constitutions of the United States and of Texas was passed; furthermore, all public school teachers had to be citizens of the United States.

Thus it was that the war years set a dangerous precedent for forced conformity, for popular approval of coercion of citizens who dared to be different. And the changes in society that followed the relaxation of war tensions brought about an extension of such activities to other fields. By 1919 many people were tired of the progressive legislation of the preceding twenty years which had attempted to change human nature by the passage of laws. The popularity of clandestine taverns (called speakeasies), the rising divorce rate, and the general loosening of morals following the end of the war reflected a fundamental change in Texas society, a reaction against a way of life that was forever gone. Yet there were still a large number of citizens who would return to the "good old days," even if it meant they had to force everyone to do so.

Still another factor which helps explain the widespread invasion of individual rights during the post-war era was the short depression that began in 1919 as war orders ceased and industrial plants began to close. Unemployed whites turned against the Negroes, a racial minority that competed for lower-paying jobs.

The feeling of "one-hundred-percent Americanism" of the war years, the popular approval of forced conformity during that time, the racial prejudice brought on by economic competition, and the longing for the moral standards of a bygone age led many citizens outside the law as they attempted to coerce their fellow Texans to conform. Those who would force everyone to be "good"

Ku Klux Klansmen

turned to such organizations as the Ku Klux Klan and such methods as the bullwhip and tar and feathers, even in some instances to "hemp justice."

The Klan of the 1920's bore no relation or connection to the organization that appeared in the South during Reconstruction. Started in 1915 in Georgia, the new Klan declared that it stood for "the preservation of law and order, protection of virtuous womanhood and orthodox Protestant moral standards, abstinence from alcoholic beverages, premarital chastity, marital fidelity, respect for parental authority, and maintenance of white supremacy." Klansmen said they stood ready to make war on corrupt officials and immoral citizens. Some members said they were helping carry out the work of the Lord by whipping "sinners," running undesirables out of town, and contributing to worthy causes. Often when a church was holding a revival, the local Klansmen would appear fully robed and masked in the church on the last night of services and present a check to the evangelist.

Such were the intentions and philosophy of the Klan; in actual practice the organization was strongly anti-Catholic, anti-Jewish, and anti-Negro. Its weapons were fear and secrecy. "The man you thought was your friend might be back-biting you to the Kluckers," wrote one Negro about the period. "A person couldn't trust nobody. Even the law was hooked up with them a lot of the time."

And the Klan often brought out worse evils than it corrected. It worked outside the law; it was judge, jury, and executioner; it sometimes punished innocent people; and it gave cowards a way to cloak their own acts with the robes of righteousness. For example, in Austin in 1921 two young men, Tom Hodges and James Hamilton, were competing for the affection of the same girl. Hamilton, a Klansman, told the secret organization that Hodges was doing evil, that he should be punished. The innocent man was waylaid, whipped almost to death, and tarred and feathered. The beating he received was so severe that he was blinded and permanently crippled in one leg. In this case, Hamilton was brought to trial, convicted, and given fifteen years in the penitentiary; but many other citizens were never punished for similar vicious deeds.

The first recorded public appearance of the new Klan in Texas was in October 1920 when a line of its hooded members marched in a Confederate veterans' parade in Houston. In the two years that followed, the organization gained a large membership, spreading its "invisible empire" to almost every corner of the state. Between 1921 and 1925 it was a strong factor, sometimes the decisive one, in every election.

Almost as a matter of course, strong opposition to the Klan developed among men of equal conviction and equal willingness to go outside the law. In South Texas the Anti-Ku Klux Klan was organized and announced that it stood for the destruction of its foe, even if it had to resort to "hot lead." Similar movements sprang up in many of the larger cities in the state, and the Klan was denounced by chambers of commerce, the Texas Bar Association, and numerous local district attorneys.

It became Governor Pat Neff's task to control the violence that was developing. Neff reached the chief executive's office after one of the hardest fought campaigns in Texas history. His major opponent for the office was none other than ex-Senator Joseph Weldon Bailey, who came out of political retirement to make the race.

In 1919 Bailey spoke to a meeting of his followers in Fort Worth, denouncing the "growing tendency to regulate everything by law," attacking the Wilson administration, and going on record against class legislation. He declared that he was still interested in Texas politics, but hoped that he would never again "have to hold public office."

Gradually he allowed his mind to be changed. His followers spoke in every part of the state of the need for Bailey's experience in Austin, and soon a flood of mail poured in on the ex-senator asking that he make the race. Bailey responded by announcing that he would be a candidate "if it becomes necessary."

On February 18, 1920, he made his formal announcement that he would seek the Democratic nomination for governor. Speaking to a crowd of four thousand at Gainesville, he declared that he had hoped "some other good citizen would enter the race" and lead the forces of democracy against the "poisonous politicalism prevailing throughout the country." Since no such individual had stepped forward, he found it necessary to do so himself. Declaring that he would "redeem Texas and Democracy," he outlined his platform: a cut in state expenditures by one-third to one-half, a reduction in taxes, better educational facilities, the separation of church and state, and less control from Washington. He denounced labor unions, nationwide prohibition, women's suffrage, the League of Nations, the Wilson administration, socialism, monopoly, and class legislation. He concluded that only he could "lead Texas back into the straight and narrow path of the time-honored principles of the old Bailey Democracy."

The ex-senator was the second man to announce his candidacy for the governorship. First was Pat Neff, a native of McGregor (a small town near Waco). A graduate of Baylor University and the law school of the University of Texas, Neff had served in the Texas legislature and was speaker of the House in the Twenty-eighth Legislature. Afterward, he became district attorney in McLennan County and then entered private law practice in Waco. In many ways Neff resembled Woodrow Wilson; he was quiet, dignified, devoutly religious, and a strong supporter of prohibition. In his opening speech Neff broke a Texas political tradition and startled the professional politicians by announcing that he had never fired a gun or baited a hook.

Two other candidates entered the race for governor: Robert Ewing Thomason and Ben F. Looney. Thomason, a native of Tennessee, made his home at Gainesville. A lawyer, he considered among his assets a widely known name and extensive public experience. Looney had been born in Louisiana but had lived for many years in Marion County, Texas. He was best known for his three terms as attorney general of the state (1913-1919).

All of Bailey's opponents were progressives, all supported Woodrow Wilson's policies, and all announced that they favored woman suffrage, national prohibition, strict law enforcement, fewer pardons for criminals, economy in state government, lower taxes, improvements of rural schools, higher teacher salaries, and nine-month school terms. Likewise all three declared themselves supporters of labor unions and collective bargaining. Neff's platform, in addition, included a highway building program of huge proportions, a system of state parks, and the conservation of water.

The first test of strength came in the Democratic state convention that convened in May 1920 to pick delegates to the Democratic national convention. Bailey's candidate as leader of the Texas delegation was Judge William Poindexter; his three opponents favored Governor Hobby. When the state convention met in Dallas, not more than

42 of the 1,409 delegates were Bailey supporters. The convention endorsed the Wilson administration, recorded itself as favoring a complete enforcement of national prohibition, and chose Hobby to head the Texas delegation.

Following this crushing defeat, Bailey left Texas without making a statement for the newspapers; he went to Washington for a two-week stay in connection with his legal practice. Many Texans predicted that the ex-senator would withdraw from the gubernatorial race, but they underestimated Bailey's love of a fight. Soon he was back in Texas campaigning harder than ever. During the last weeks before the primary election, Bailey renewed his attacks on labor unions, declared that women voters had defeated him in the May convention in their deluded belief that he was trying to bring whiskey back, and criticized Neff for the enthusiastic support he was receiving from the Baptists. The ex-senator declared that Baptist ministers were using their pulpits as campaign platforms for Neff.

Neff retorted by challenging Bailey to a series of debates on the issues, but Bailey refused, declaring that such debates would only lead to criticism of personalities.

In 1918 Texas election laws had been amended to provide for a runoff primary for all offices—state, district, and local—when no candidate received a majority vote. Since there had only been two candidates for governor that year, no runoff had been necessary. In 1920 each of the four contenders was predicting that he would be in the runoff; Neff, Thomason, and Looney each conceded that Bailey would be his opponent in the second primary.

And the three were correct in assuming that Bailey would be in the runoff. The statewide vote was Bailey

152,340; Neff, 149,818; Thomason, 99,022; and Looney, 48,640. Bailey found his greatest strength in South and Southwest Texas, while Neff had led generally in the counties of North and West Texas.

With the field narrowed to only two candidates, the tempo increased considerably. Ex-Senator Bailey continued to use the same tactics he had followed in the first primary, criticizing the Wilson program, complaining of the many innovations and extensions of the federal government, and pleading for a return of the old-fashioned way of life. At Denton he deplored the replacement of church organs with immense pipe instruments. He declared that modern dances, such as the "fox trot" and the "bunny hug," were too strenuous for women and that society should return to the waltz and square dances. He added that he found equally distasteful the new songs such as "Oh, You Great Big Beautiful Doll" and "I Love My Wife, But Oh You Kid." Plaintively Bailey said he preferred "Swanee River" and "My Old Kentucky Home."

Neff poked fun at Bailey's nostalgic longing for the old songs and dances, declaring that his opponent was opposed to the twentieth century, that Baileyism represented stagnation and reaction. From the *Congressional Record* he read a speech made years earlier by the ex-senator in which Bailey had proposed that automobiles be denied the use of Washington streets because they were dangerous and frightened horses. Using Bailey's voting record, Neff charged that his opponent was opposed to the buying and selling of Liberty Bonds, that he stood for open saloons, and that he had fought woman suffrage, the Federal Farm Loan Act, child labor laws, the 1920 Democratic national platform, and the Democratic nominee for President, James M. Cox. He even charged that Bailey, who had lived the past eight years in Washington, was no longer a Texas citizen and therefore was ineligible for the governorship.

At last the runoff election returns were in and showed that Neff had defeated his opponent by 264,075 to 184,702. Bailey, who carried only 46 of the 250 counties that reported, received approximately forty percent of the popular vote. The press reported that the ex-senator was too astonished to comment on his defeat, his first at the hands of the voters of Texas. One friend declared that the election of 1920 aged Bailey by twenty years. Later, however, the ex-senator issued a statement in which he said that even in defeat he was consoled by the fact that he had made an honest effort to rescue the Democratic party from the control of those who were seeking to destroy it.

Neff reacted to his victory by a statement of appreciation and gratitude for the confidence of his friends and the voters. In the November general election that followed, he easily defeated token Republican opposition. The only noteworthy part of the general election was James E. Ferguson's bid for the presidency of the United States.

In August 1919 Ferguson announced the formation of his own political organization, the American Party, and declared himself a candidate for President. Speaking before a Labor Day crowd at Thurber, Texas, in 1920, he thundered at his audience in his old style: "Step by step we have seen our liberties taken from us, and we wonder what will come next. . . . Freedom in business gone. Freedom in pleasure gone. Freedom in government gone. Man has begun to resent the unwarranted trespass upon his rights, and from every hill and hamlet, from every shop and shed, from every town and village we can hear the murmuring multitude. . . ." Still there was not enough of a reaction to elect him to the high office he sought; he received only about sixty thousand votes. Probably Ferguson did not expect to win. He merely meant to keep his name before the voters of the state.

Governor Neff upon taking office revealed his genuine sympathy with the forces of reform. He even refused to hold an inauguration ball because as a Baptist he did not believe in dancing. His immediate concern was halting the crime wave then prevalent in the state as Klansmen took matters into their own hands. Neff called upon the Thirty-seventh Legislature to pass a law authorizing the attorney general to remove any officer who was dishonest, inefficient, or indifferent in the performance of his duties. But the legislature was not in sympathy with the high moral tone of the new governor's administration and disregarded his repeated calls for stricter law enforcement measures. Likewise, they paid no heed to his recommendations for improvement in the state prison system, better labor conditions, rural school improvements, a better public health program, the conservation of water, and protection of overflow lands.

The only major bill to pass the regular session of 1921 was one reapportioning seats for the legislature, but Neff considered the reapportionment unfair to the west and vetoed the bill. In the second called session another reapportionment act passed providing for new congressional, senatorial, and representative districts. It received the approval of the governor.

The uncooperative Thirty-seventh Legislature adjourned without making an appropriation to run the state government. The first called session did likewise, bringing from the governor the charge that the legislators were adjourning without passing appropriations bills merely to force him to call special meetings in order that the legislators might collect their mileage and per diem allowances. Finally Neff got the appropriation bill he wanted. Two and one-half million dollars were set aside for rural school aid; additional funds were provided for vocational training in the public schools; and the University of Texas was voted $1,300,000 for enlarging its campus. Other bills signed into law by the governor included such measures as state licensing and supervision of maternity homes, the regulation and licensing of optometrists by a newly created board, the building of a tubercular hospital at Kerrville for ex-soldiers, and allowing cities to build public hospitals.

Aside from his difficulties with the legislature during his first term, Neff was confronted with a railroad strike that threatened to bring transportation to a halt in the state. The governor reacted by declaring martial law at Denison and other centers of labor difficulty and thereby forced a settlement on the unions. His action met with the approval of the public, but brought a hostile feeling toward him from organized labor for his "interference."

Opponents of the Neff administration began as early as the fall of 1921 to seek a candidate who might defeat him for reelection. They held about a hundred conferences in different parts of the state, but they found few politicians or private citizens willing to make a contest against the man who had defeated Joe Bailey by almost a hundred thousand votes. Therefore, in the election of 1922, only political unknowns opposed Neff's bid for the traditional second term. Fred S. Rogers, a farmer and labor leader from Bonham, was the leading contender in the Democratic primary. Opening his campaign in Sulphur Springs in April 1922 before a crowd of three thousand, Rogers criticized the Neff administration for extravagance and inefficiency and deplored the "preventable" inadequacy of rural education in Texas. Later in his spirited campaign, Rogers took up the charge that Neff was in sympathy with the Ku Klux Klan.

Governor Neff seemed indifferent to the various candidates and did not announce his candidacy for reelection until less than a month before the primary. His campaign was dignified and colorless; never once did he mention by name any of his opponents. He defended his administration against its critics and declared that his first-hand experience with the state's problems qualified him to solve them. Although he published no formal platform, he urged the people when electing legislators to consider the need for law enforcement legislation, prison reforms, aid to the public schools, flood control, highway building, taxation, and labor.

In the July primary Neff was nominated without a runoff. He received a majority of some fifty thousand votes over all his opponents combined. Rogers ran second, trailing the governor by about 130,000 votes.

The contest that really thrilled the voters of Texas in the Democratic primary of 1922 was that one to select a United States senator. Since the office was a federal one, Ferguson's enemies could not keep his name off the ballot and he announced for the seat. Incumbent Charles A. Culberson, who had held the seat for more than twenty years, was standing for reelection, but he was too elderly and too ill to be a real contender. In spite of his outstanding record, the younger generation of voters did not know him. Political experts in Texas picked Earle B. Mayfield, a lawyer, former member of the legislature, and a railroad commissioner, as the likeliest candidate. Three other politicians were making spirited bids to replace Culberson, but it was Ferguson who startled Texans when it was announced that he had run second to Mayfield in the first primary, thus gaining a place in the runoff. In the second primary the major issue between the two candidates was the Ku Klux Klan. Mayfield admitted having been a member, and he received the endorsement and support of the secret organization. Ferguson thundered against the Klan and its brand of "swamp justice." In return the ex-governor was heckled by Klansmen at almost every rally he attended, but they never dared lay a hand on him. After a spirited contest, the pro-Klan and anti-Ferguson voters swept Mayfield into office by 317,591 to 265,233. Farmer Jim had missed being "vindicated," but he was far from finished in Texas politics.

Governor Neff's message to the Thirty-eighth Legislature, which met in January 1923, was progressive and statesmanlike. Once again he called for strong law enforcement statutes, requesting the passage of an act to provide for the removal of incompetent officers. He quoted crime statistics to show that in 1922 Texas, with a population of five million, had over a thousand murders, while London, with eight million people, had only twenty-four homicides. "The operation of the criminal law in Texas is a disgrace to the state," he declared.

He also spoke at some length on the need of a revision of the Constitution of 1876, a document he termed outmoded and obsolete. And he submitted a plan for fundamental and far-reaching changes in the state's educational system, including the authorization of a state board of education, the appropriation of larger sums of money for the schools, the guarantee of nine months of school for each child per year, and a definite income for the colleges in order that they might avoid the "biennial political wrangling for funds."

But the legislature was not greatly impressed with the

governor's progressive program and took little action. The proposal to submit the question of a constitutional convention to the voters was ignored, and no important changes were made in the laws for educational facilities. The legislature did provide that county judges could remove drunken, incompetent, or uncooperative peace officers, but made a mockery of the statute by appending a proviso that intoxication was no cause for dismissal when the official was drinking liquor prescribed by a licensed physician. Neff's reform demands appeared to have been made in vain.

The major fireworks in the Thirty-eighth Legislature came when Ferguson supporters in the Senate, including Archie Parr of San Diego, Joe Burkett of Eastland, and I. D. Fairchild of Lufkin, attempted to get Ferguson's political rights restored. They had planned their strategy well in advance and therefore were ready to act when on February 9, 1923, Lieutenant Governor T. Whitfield Davidson, a bitter Ferguson foe, stepped down temporarily as presiding officer in the upper house, leaving Parr in charge. Parr immediately recognized Burkett who introduced Senate Resolution 57 calling for the removal from the Senate records of the impeachment proceedings against Ferguson and a restoration of Ferguson's right to hold office in Texas. Parr then called for a voice vote on the resolution, banged his gavel, and declared that the bill had passed. Senator Fairchild thereupon jumped to his feet and moved for adjournment. Another voice vote was taken, and again Parr declared that the "ayes" were in the majority.

The plan had been faultlessly executed, and a howl of protest arose from the anti-Ferguson members of the chamber. One of the Ferguson opponents rushed to tell Lieutenant Governor Davidson the news of what had happened. Davidson reconvened the Senate, recognized a Ferguson foe who moved that the record of all that had transpired since the lieutenant governor left the presiding chair be expunged from the record, called for a voice vote, and declared that the new motion had carried. The ex-governor was once again denied the right to hold public office.

The next morning's headlines in the Fort Worth *Star-Telegram* best summed up the episode: "Ferguson Citizen for 30 Minutes!"

As time for the 1924 primary election grew near, Ferguson went to court in a vain attempt to win the right of having his named carried on the Democratic ballot. Failing that, he hit upon the expedient of running his wife, Miriam A. Ferguson, for the office. Politicians gave a stunned gasp when the story broke in the newspapers; then an amused chuckle filled the air. No one considered "Ma" (her initials were M. A.) a serious threat in the approaching primary.

The other major candidates in the race were Judge Felix D. Robertson of Dallas, who had the strong support of the Klan; Lynch Davidson, a Houston businessman and lumber tycoon; and T. Whitfield Davidson, the lieutenant governor. Political experts predicted that Judge Robertson would win, perhaps without a runoff, but they reckoned without the fiery oratory and political astuteness of Jim Ferguson and the rising public discontent with the high-handed tactics of the Klan.

Ferguson rallies usually opened with Mrs. Ferguson's making a short, simple plea to the women of the state to help her clear her family's name. "A vote for me is a vote of confidence for my husband, who cannot be a candidate because his enemies have succeeded in barring him from holding public office," she would say. Then she would admit that she was no orator and introduce "Pa," as he came to be called.

In the first primary Ferguson concentrated his attacks on the hooded riders who were terrorizing the state. "We will take the courts out of the swamps and put them back in the courthouse where they should be," he promised. In thunderous tones he denounced Judge Robertson, the "Klan's Klandidate." To charges that Mrs. Ferguson would merely be a figurehead governor for him, Ferguson disarmingly replied with a twinkle in his eyes that such might be the case but that Texas thereby could have "Two Governors For the Price of One." He declared that his wife would cut state expenditures by fifteen million dollars a year. And he ridiculed his opponents' platforms, saying they were "like the hoop skirt which covers everything and touches nothing."

Both Lynch Davidson and T. Whitfield Davidson made aggressive campaigns, each flaying the Klan wherever possible. Lynch Davidson had the support of more than a hundred newspapers, made more than two hundred speeches, and was considered the likeliest opponent of Robertson in the runoff.

Judge Robertson, seemingly assured of victory, carried on a dignified campaign in the first primary. He declared the real issues in the election were three in number: law enforcement, public education, and economy in government. He promised, if elected, to cut expenses and taxes and spoke often of the need for more religion in public and private life. His slogan, he said, was "common sense, common honesty, and Christianity." His program included prison reform and reestablishment of the Pardons Board which had been disbanded by Neff. Judge Robertson was not a polished orator and had little to recommend him to the voters except his Klan affiliation and support and his repeated insistence that he was a dedicated prohibitionist.

On July 26 the people went to the polls. As the returns came in during the first evening, Judge Robertson had a commanding lead, followed by Lynch Davidson and Miriam Ferguson. On the second and third days following the election, the rural vote began to trickle in, bringing Mrs. Ferguson's total even with and then past that of Lynch Davidson. The final tally was Robertson, 193,508; Ferguson, 146,424; Lynch Davidson, 141,208; and T. Whitfield Davidson, 125,011. Mrs. Ferguson had made the runoff.

With the first primary out of the way, the remaining two candidates began to fight seriously. Judge Robertson turned his attention to Ferguson's record as governor, labelling him a "traitor" and the greatest grafter in the country. Robertson said the voters of the state should go to the polls and vindicate Texas for impeaching Ferguson, rather than go to the polls and vindicate the ex-governor as Ferguson was asking.

Mrs. Ferguson had little trouble getting all the publicity any candidate could want. The fact that she had made the runoff brought newspapermen from as far away as New York City; each one wanted stories and pictures. She posed peeling peaches, wearing sunbonnets, feeding the chickens, and hoeing her garden. Her husband was always at hand to see that each reporter got what he wanted. Another part of the Ferguson campaign was the stickers that appeared around the state on automobile bumpers and not a few wagons, proclaiming, "Me For Ma." Some of them added, "And I Ain't Got a Dern Thing Against Pa."

The Klan issue grew to such proportions in the race that the contest between Mrs. Ferguson and Judge Robertson became a referendum; the people were voting not so much for a candidate as for or against the Klan. And there could be no fence-sitting. Friends of Robertson approached ex-Senator Joe Bailey soliciting support for their man. Bailey had long hated Jim Ferguson, but he replied that he would vote for Ma as "the only way I [can] register my protest against the Klan effectively." Other influential citizens, including the editor of the Dallas *News* and former Attorney General M. M. Crane, made the same difficult choice: Fergusonism or the Klan.

Tension mounted to almost unbearable heights before the runoff was conducted. When the results were finally announced, many Texans could not believe what the voters of their state had done—the nominee of the Democratic party for the governorship was a woman. Mrs. Ferguson had won! Or was it that the Klan had lost? The vote was 413,751 to 316,019; Mrs. Ferguson carried 173 of the 249 counties that reported returns.

But the Klan and the anti-Ferguson voters were not willing to give up without another fight. In a last-ditch attempt to prevent the Fergusons from returning to the governor's mansion, they rallied to the support of the candidate of the Republican party, Dr. George C. Butte, dean of the law school of the University of Texas. Butte made a spirited bid for the office, speaking extensively over the state, urging Democrats to desert the party of their fathers and vote Republican in the general election. He argued that the real issue of the election was responsible government, that should Mrs. Ferguson win the state would be at the mercy of Jim Ferguson, a man whose public record had been tried and found wanting.

Butte drew large audiences, and his supporters began claiming that he would carry San Antonio, West Texas, and the race itself. Lending a voice in behalf of the Republican candidate was Will Hobby and the Houston *Post-Dispatch,* editorially declaring that Butte was sounding a "note of lofty idealism that is not often heard in latter-day politics."

The strong Republican campaign rallied a diverse group of Democrats to the support of their party and their candidate. And James Ferguson was as indefatigable as ever, stumping up and down the state with his old style and vigor. It was a contest without humor, a mudslinging battle that involved personalities, a race that inflamed tempers and produced endless fights.

At last election day arrived. Mrs. Ferguson received 422,528 votes, Butte 294,970. The Republican had lost, but he had made the best showing since Reconstruction days for a member of his party.

The new governor kept her word about the Klan. One of her first acts upon taking office was to ask the legislature to pass a law making it a criminal offense to wear a mask in public. The legislature, perhaps feeling that Mrs. Ferguson's election as an anti-Klan candidate signified the people's desire to be rid of the nightriders, complied with her request. The anti-mask law proved a deathblow to the Klan. Thereafter the Ku Klux Klan dwindled to a negligible force in Texas politics and social life, eventually withering away completely.

As much as the Fergusons hated and fought the Klan, however, they should have been grateful for it. Through the fight against the organization, James Ferguson was finally vindicated. Mrs. Ferguson could say, as they pulled their car to a halt before the governor's mansion, "We departed in disgrace; we now return in glory."

6

The Booming Twenties

ON THE HIGH PLAINS of West Texas, two farmers stood
watching in awe as water gushed forth in a steady stream
from an irrigation well, a new and startling aid to agriculture in the region. One of the men was a newcomer
to the area; the other had lived there many years.

"But is there enough water under there for this irrigation to last?" asked the skeptical newcomer.

"The way I see it," replied the old-timer, "this land
we're standing on is just a crust over a great big under-
ground lake. The only thing I worry about is that the
land might break loose and sink with us."

What these two men were witnessing was the beginning
of a revolution, one that is still continuing. The water
produced by irrigation meant that an area once labelled

[93]

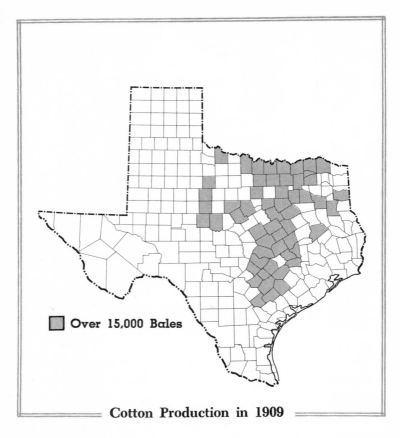

Over 15,000 Bales

Cotton Production in 1909

in the geography books as "The Great American Desert"
would become the agricultural wonder of the world; it
meant that on the High Plains cattle would gradually be
replaced by fields of cotton, sorghum, and wheat that
stretched from horizon to horizon; it meant that great
ranches would be broken up into smaller tracts and sold
to land-hungry farmers; it meant that land prices would
soar from ten dollars an acre to seven and eight hundred
dollars an acre; it meant that mechanical farming could

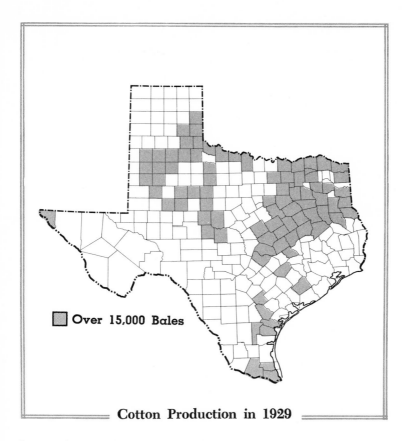

Over 15,000 Bales

Cotton Production in 1929

be profitably conducted because machinery could be efficiently used on the level, treeless plains. It was irrigation
water that transformed the "desert" into flourishing farmland.

Some farming had been conducted on the High Plains
even before the first irrigation well was drilled. A few
hardy pioneers took advantge of the seasonal rains to
raise small crops, using special techniques known as "dry-
land farming," but their efforts met with only limited

success and were closely tied to the weather. The changes brought by irrigation may best be seen from Department of Agriculture figures which reveal that in 1918 only 50,588 bales of cotton were grown in West Texas; just eight years later the figure was 1,130,713 bales. Acres under cultivation jumped from 45,101 in 1909 to 2,334,393 in 1924.

Most of this expansion took place in what came to be known as the South Plains, the area surrounding the city of Lubbock. The increase was brought about by low prices for land, fertile soil, and a comparative absence of insect pests. The boll weevil, the scourge of East and Central Texas cotton farmers, was almost powerless in much of the plains country because of the colder winters. And mechanical farming, the fruit of the industrial revolution, came into its own at last. Land was broken with tractors and gang-plows. The cotton was planted with two-row planters and cultivated with two-row cultivators. Often the laborious process of chopping cotton—thinning the crop with a hoe—was entirely omitted, for the machinery could be adjusted to space the seeds properly as they were planted. At harvest time the crop was frequently gathered with a cotton sled or a mechanical picker. Thus it was that the cost of production was less than in other parts of the South.

The same advantages held true for wheat. All but one of the eleven counties producing more than a half million bushels of this commodity in Texas in 1924 were in West Texas. Oats developed as another important grain crop in the region, as did milo-maize, kafir corn, feterita, hegari ("high-gear"), and several varieties of cane. These sorghum crops, which commanded much acreage because of their drouth resistance, constituted the chief feed crop on most of the farms where animals were kept.

Despite this increase in agricultural activity in West Texas during the 1920's, the area was still known primarily as a rancher's paradise. Yet the ranching industry was undergoing relatively rapid and fundamental changes, due largely to the unfavorable conditions which prevailed in the cattle and livestock market from 1920 to 1927. There were 2,068,768 head of cattle in West Texas in 1920; just five years later the number had declined to 1,739,476. Many ranches were abandoned entirely after 1920. Windmills were torn down and hauled off, and millions of acres of range land were allowed to lie idle. Gradually these acres were broken up and sold to the farmers. Stock-raising, however, did not die out completely; a few large ranches remained in the broken country along the Canadian River, and many farmers moving into the area bought cattle to fatten for market on grain and forage crops which they raised.

The large-scale ranchers began shifting their activities to the Edwards Plateau, to the Trans-Pecos area, or to the coastal plains south and southwest of San Antonio. The Trans-Pecos region and the Edwards Plateau were considered in the 1920's to be permanent ranching country. Rainfall in these areas was usually less than eighteen inches per year, the land was uneven, the topsoil was shallow and sterile, and field crops grew poorly. Grazing seemed to be the most economical and profitable use for both regions. One noteworthy change taking place in Texas during the twenties, especially in the Edwards Plateau, was an increased production of sheep and goats. High prices for wool, mutton, and mohair attracted many cattlemen to this type of ranching, and the number of sheep and goats in Texas increased rapidly.

In South Texas the cattlemen were not as successful, for once again they found themselves in sharp competition with the farmers for land. Irrigation water from the Rio Grande made cotton farming possible in the region, and thousands of bales were marketed annually from that region. But it was the introduction of a new crop—citrus fruit—that caused land prices to soar in the Lower Rio Grande Valley.

Prior to the 1920's no great amount of space had been devoted to citrus groves; early in the decade, however, it became widely known that the industry had real possibilities, and many people from the Middle West rushed to the region to buy land. In 1925 the *Texas Almanac* reported that there were 750,000 citrus fruit trees in the Lower Rio Grande Valley and declared that the number was increasing rapidly. Most of the trees were young; consequently, shipments that year were light. On all sides, however, predictions for the future were bright.

These remarkable changes in Texas agriculture went largely unnoticed, because of the even more startling developments in the cities and towns. In the months and years following World War I, it was easy to see that Texas, along with the rest of the United States, had entered an era that was quite different from the older, less hectic way of life. "A new age," Governor Will Hobby termed the period in 1919. "A turning point in civilization" was Pat Neff's assessment just two years later.

And it was a new age—one of rapid changes. During the decade following the return of Texas' fighting men from the war fronts, there was an increasing demand for higher education, highway construction went forward at a rapid rate, and business was booming. Everywhere the fruits of the industrial revolution were ripening.

During the twenties young men and women came more

and more to realize the value, even the necessity, of a higher education. As a result of the increasing number of students, new colleges were created and the older ones increased their enrollments; for example, in 1925 Texas Technological College first opened its doors in Lubbock to be greeted by an enrollment of more than one thousand students.

Mile after mile of new hard-surfaced highways were constructed to provide roads for the large number of automobiles that Texans purchased. Because the state was so large and the cost of building such roads so high, new taxes had to be imposed. Working on the theory that the users of the highways should pay for their construction, the legislature began imposing a tax on gasoline in 1933, gradually raising it to four cents a gallon, three cents to be used for building roads, one cent for education. State funds were matched by money from the federal government, and millions of dollars were spent. Gradually Texas developed one of the best highway systems in the nation, but not without charges of fraud and corruption during the early years.

The most remarkable feature of the twenties in Texas was the development of industry. New manufacturing plants were built in record numbers; lumbering became a major industry, with paper mills employing hundreds of workers and turning out newsprint, wood products, and fine paper; sulfur production doubled and redoubled, from dome deposits along the coast which were soon yielding eighty percent of the nation's supply of sulfur; meat-packing plants in Fort Worth and other Texas cities were built or modernized to process cattle and hogs from the ranches and farms for the dining tables of a hungry nation; public utility companies, organized in great numbers to bring electric power to the cities, towns, and even farms, generated power through burning oil, natural gas, or Texas lignite coal.

All this business activity was overshadowed, however, by a second spectacular boom of oil activity. Just as the discovery of the Spindletop field brought about speculation and company organization, so the opening of the Ranger Field in Eastland County in 1917 led to another feverish rush to partake of the riches associated with "black gold." Following the Ranger discovery, oil was found in Wichita County at the Burkburnett Field in 1919, the Mexia Field in Limestone County in 1920, near Luling in 1922, the Big Lake Field in Reagan County in 1923, and the Wortham Field in 1924-1925. Coupled with this activity was a comeback at Spindletop in 1925 when the field was extended south and its output increased to a greater number of barrels than the original field had produced. But the greatest story of petroleum activity in Texas during the twenties, just as with agriculture, was written in the Panhandle.

The Panhandle area discovery is usually dated in 1921, but a great amount of study and even a few discoveries preceded that year. As early as 1905 Charles N. Gould, a geologist from the University of Oklahoma, began preliminary surveys in Potter, Moore, Sherman, and Dallam counties, then worked along Trujillo Creek in western Oldham County, finally completing the season's work with an examination of the formations in Palo Duro Canyon.

In 1916 Dr. Gould, by then a consulting geologist in Oklahoma City, revisited the region and was persuaded to make surveys and map the area. Following another investigation, Dr. Gould announced that he had found a favorable area some thirty miles from Amarillo. As a result M. C. Nobles, a wholesale grocer in Amarillo, joined with associates and formed the Amarillo Oil Company, leasing approximately seventy thousand acres lying on both sides of the Canadian River. Their first well was completed in December 1918 at a cost of $70,000 and produced not oil but gas—ten million cubic feet a day— which its sponsors soon piped to Amarillo. The company subsequently drilled eight other wells, one of them (the No. 4 Masterson) a 107,000,000 cubic-feet-a-day well. Only one of the nine failed to produce gas.

These discoveries of gas caused great excitement and satisfaction in Amarillo. During the five years following 1919 some 114 companies were organized in the city, selling most of their stock to local buyers for twelve million dollars. It was later discovered that more than two thirds of those twelve million dollars was paid for worthless stock.

None of the first Panhandle drillers and organizers realized the enormous extent of the producing area. Only when oil and gas wells began to dot the prairies in an unbroken line for mile after mile did geologists begin to speak of the great size of the find. When maps were finally compiled, they revealed a 115-mile-long producing zone that crossed Wheeler, Gray, Carson, Hutchinson, Potter, and Moore counties. Production figures for 1926 showed an output of 25,551,000 barrels. Helping swell this total was the Borger Field which opened on January 11, 1926, when the Dixon Creek Oil and Refining Company brought in a ten-thousand-barrel-a-day oil well. The same year also saw the beginning of the Pampa Field when Shamrock Oil Company brought in its first well.

As a result of this oil activity, towns boomed at a fantastic rate. The census of 1920 listed the population of Amarillo as 15,494; in January 1927 the Newspaper Feature Service estimated the town had grown to 52,680. Assessed property evaluation jumped ten million dollars in one year, while in the same period bank deposits more than doubled. And the same was true for the other towns in the Panhandle.

A spectacular example of the way towns grew occurred about fifty miles east of Amarillo. Following the discovery of an oil field there in January 1926, A. P. Borger, an Oklahoma townsite promoter, moved into the region and bought 240 acres on which he laid out a town and began selling lots. Soon the main street was two miles long and lined with clapboard shacks, tents, and buildings of every type. Businesses dotted the thoroughfare in chaotic fashion: rooming houses and hotels, dance halls and pool rooms, hot-dog stands and chili parlors, and reputable businesses such as a bank, a barber shop, and hardware stores. Within months after its founding, Borger had a population estimated at between ten and twenty thousand, including oil field workers and their families, "con" men and gamblers, speculators and promoters. It was a wild town described by one visitor as a "rootin'-tootin', snortin', hell-raisin' place." Finally, the Texas Rangers had to come in and force Borger's citizens to become orderly, just as the famed organization had done at Ranger and Mexia previously.

Another area of significant discoveries in the midtwenties was in West Texas where fields were opened in Crane, Upton, Yates, and Winkler counties. Here the discovery of petroleum had similar results: related industries came to the region, population expanded, and cities grew. McCamey changed from a quiet cowtown to a booming city of ten thousand within a few months after the first oil well came in; Crane County, which had a population of fourteen as late as 1918, increased sufficiently in population for a county government to be organized; Colorado City, Big Spring, Midland, Odessa, and Pecos

City (now Pecos) were transformed by the influx of oil field workers. There was an epidemic of hotel building in the region as the former "wide places in the road" had their streets paved and built 150- and 200-room hotels which usually were filled to capacity. Many new towns stood where only a few years before cattle had grazed on the open range. Ranchers and farmers in the vicinity benefitted from royalty and lease payments, and soon it became fashionable for these families to maintain two residences, a "town house" and the homestead in the country.

With all of this production added to the volume from other fields, Texas in 1928, for the first time in history, led all other states in the volume of oil pumped from the earth; the total that year was 256,888,000 barrels. The entire world production that year was 1,322,896,000 barrels. P. R. MacIntosh, an oil expert at that time, pointed out that the West Texas fields contained the largest oil reserve of any area on the North American continent and probably in the world.

To get this oil to market, Texas refineries and pipelines were being built at a rapid clip. In 1919 there were 43 refineries operating in the state with a combined capacity of 277,200 barrels daily; by 1928 the number had jumped to 101 with a total capacity of 750,000 barrels daily. In 1918 there were 3,116 miles of trunk pipelines in the entire state; during 1927 and 1928 more than 5,500 miles of pipeline were laid in West Texas alone—across mountains and deserts that presented unusual construction difficulties—sometimes the work was done far from a railroad, necessitating the building of roads so that materials and workers could be brought in by truck. The Pasotex Petroleum Company, which laid an 8-inch line the 195 miles from Winkler County to its refinery at El Paso, surmounted extreme problems. The pipe ran up and over the mountains near Guadalupe Peak, the highest point in Texas, and in one place spanned a canyon on an eight-thousand-foot-long trestle.

By the late 1920's petroleum and petroleum products were undoubtedly the greatest factor in the economy of Texas. The income from oil and gas contributed heavily to the deposits in Texas banks and to the assets of insurance companies; it built many of the skyscrapers dotting the state's cities; and it produced a large part of the income that sustained department stores and other business institutions. Farmers and ranchers were enriched through rents and royalties, workers in the petroleum industry received salaries, and Texas as a whole benefitted.

Such a giant factor in the state's economy did not escape the notice of the government, and there was increasing taxation for the benefit of the highway program and for the educational system. When Miriam Ferguson went before the Thirty-ninth Legislature in 1925, she referred to the two-million-dollar deficiency in the general revenue fund, to the expected revenue of thirty-eight million dollars for the coming biennium, and to the forty-three million dollars that had been requested as appropriations for the coming two-year period. To meet this situation, the governor called for economy, reform, and new taxes.

She requested an increase in the state gasoline tax which had been established at one cent a gallon in 1923, and she also suggested a small tax on the sales of tobacco from which she estimated four million dollars would be raised annually; this money, she felt, should be used for higher education.

In other matters Mrs. Ferguson in her message to the

legislature called for an investigation of the Banking Department, which she said was in a deplorable condition, and she asked that the duties of the Insurance Department be clarified.

Besides the anti-mask law, which was passed and curbed the activities of the Ku Klux Klan, the governor suggested that the number of Texas Rangers be decreased. "Strengthen the laws against murder, robbery, excessive speeding, and the illegal sale of liquor. Follow the suggestion of the Democratic state convention and put the bootleg drug stores out of business," she told the legislators. Referring to crowded prison conditions, the new governor declared, "I shall adopt a most liberal policy in the matter of pardons."

Mrs. Ferguson got very little of what she asked, for the Thirty-ninth Legislature ignored most of her suggestions and demands. No new taxes were levied, no new bureaus were established, and no laws of unusual interest or great importance were enacted. The proposed tax on tobacco never got out of legislative committee; nothing was done to curb liquor sales by drug stores; and the four million dollars voted by the House to supplement the available school fund failed to win approval in the Senate. The two houses did agree on an appropriation bill during the regular session, one that kept within the bounds of expected revenues. This feat was so unusual that it was hailed by the newspapers, lauded by the governor, and boasted about by the lawmakers.

With a Ferguson once again in the governor's mansion, few, if any, Texas voters expected a quiet two years; and gossips around the state capital were not disappointed. Rumors were soon circulating about certain practices and policies of the administration.

During the first twenty months of her term, Mrs. Ferguson issued more than two thousand grants of executive clemency. Her wholesale use of the pardoning power aroused questions, criticism, and condemnation from thousands of citizens. Newspapers explained the governor's liberal policy by asserting that her husband had convinced her that Governor Neff had imprisoned thousands of Ferguson supporters simply for being against prohibition. On the other hand, a story which was widely circulated—and which certainly hurt her in her 1926 bid for reelection whether true or not—concerned the visit of the father of a convicted criminal to James Ferguson's office. The father kept pleading for the ex-governor to intercede with "Ma" and get a pardon for his son; Ferguson reportedly kept changing the subject to a horse which he had for sale for the ridiculous price of five thousand dollars. The man kept talking about his son; Ferguson kept talking about his horse. Finally the father in exasperation demanded, "What on earth would I want with a five-thousand-dollar horse?"

According to the story Ferguson replied, "Well, I figure your son might ride him home from the penitentiary if you bought him."

This anecdote and others caused the Thirty-ninth Legislature to appoint a joint committee to investigate the situation. After some study the committee reported that many of Mrs. Ferguson's pardons had been granted on the recommendations of her husband, some even before the criminal could reach the state prison. But the investigation resulted in no fundamental changes.

Even more criticism and veiled charges were levelled at the Fergusons in connection with the highway construction program. Critics asserted that any company building roads for the state had to buy advertising space at very exorbitant prices in the *Ferguson Forum* if it wished to continue getting contracts to construct highways. A House committee of the Thirty-ninth Legislature investigated the charges, but ex-Governor Ferguson sat with it and dominated its actions to such an extent that nothing was accomplished.

Despite the legislative inquiry, charges continued to be made that contracts for highway construction were let on the basis of personal friendship and favoritism rather than in the best interests of the state. Louis Wiltz Kemp, then a young engineer but later to become one of Texas' most honored non-professional historians, and Don Hampton Biggers, a vituperative, free-lance journalist, exposed and publicized a number of such scandals. Attorney General Dan Moody, a crusading young lawyer, possibly with an eye to honest government or possibly to political advancement, conducted his own investigation and unearthed the corruption that actually existed. As a result of his own studies and those of his staff, Moody brought suit on behalf of the state against the American Road Company and the Hoffman Construction Company, declaring that these firms were scheduled to be paid more than seven million dollars for road building that would cost them less than two million dollars. The contracts with these two companies and with several others were soon cancelled or modified because of Moody's actions.

Besides advising his wife and working closely with the highway department, Ferguson was influential in other affairs of the state while Mrs. Ferguson occupied the governor's chair. He sat in conferences with various state boards, agencies, and commissions and enjoyed an influence as a private citizen never before achieved in the state's history. Anyone who wished to do business with the government soon learned the wisdom of securing the ex-governor's friendship and recommendation. Ferguson opponents—and they were numerous—charged that many plans, schemes, and devices were employed by businessmen in their efforts to gain Ferguson's favor.

Attorney General Dan Moody spoke out against such practices, calling the Ferguson influence "government by proxy," and in his announcement for governor in March 1926 promised to rid the state of "Fergusonism." Moody, a native of Williamson County, had been appointed district attorney of the Twenty-sixth Judicial District, which included Austin, by Governor Pat Neff and had served in that capacity from 1922 to 1925. As a district attorney Moody had gained a statewide reputation as a prosecutor of the Ku Klux Klan. In 1924 he was the successful candidate for the office of attorney general, to which he was elected at the age of thirty-one.

In announcing his candidacy for governor, Moody levelled all the current charges against Jim Ferguson and promised to bring to justice "those responsible for the inroads into the public treasury through the letting of excessive and inconscionable contracts." He pledged if elected to restore honesty in the state government, to appoint capable officials, to enforce the laws, to curtail the issuance of pardons, to put the state prison system on an efficient basis, to encourage a system of connected highways, to maintain the public schools effectively, to support higher education, and to work for judicial reform.

During his campaign, however, Moody rarely referred to his platform, insisting instead that the real issue before the voters was Fergusonism. Across the state he stumped, deriding at every stop the Fergusons' claim that their administration represented economy and efficiency. During the course of these speeches, Moody asserted that Ferguson was the salaried employee of a railroad company while serving as his wife's chief advisor, that he actually directed the program of the State Highway Commission, and that the ex-governor directed the awarding of contracts by the textbook commission, contracts involving millions of dollars of state money.

Mrs. Ferguson announced for reelection, and as in 1924 the real work of her campaigning was done by her husband. Ferguson likewise spoke all over Texas, belittling the Moody candidacy, charging the youthful attorney general with incompetence, inexperience, and unfitness. He referred to Moody as "a candidate with nothing to recommend him save a lipstick, a new wife, and a big head." He called his wife's opponent an "upstart" and a "contemptible demagogue." To emphasize Moody's youthfulness, Ferguson in one speech read a record of the grades the attorney general had made in school.

Moody retaliated by reminding the voters of Ferguson's impeachment:

> I have held three public offices in this state, and I have never been hauled before the bar of any court of justice for misconduct in any of them. I am grateful that no decree of any high court of impeachment forbids the candidacy I am now presenting. No court has ever found me guilty of application to my own use of money belonging to the people of Texas, of taking the state's money from banks that were paying interest on it and putting it in banks in which I had stock. . . . It may be that I have no peculiar qualifications for the office of governor, but at least I have never been forbidden by any court of impeachment from holding any office of honor, trust, or profit in Texas.

Driving home his point, the attorney general declared that the best remedy for Fergusonism was education. He insisted that the administration of the Fergusons had been "utterly barren of achievements and cluttered with the bones of unfilled pledges."

As time for the Democratic primary grew near, Mrs. Ferguson grew overconfident. Speaking before a crowd of seven thousand at Sulphur Springs on May 22, she said, "I will agree that if he leads me one vote in the primary, I will immediately resign without waiting until next year, if he will agree that if I lead him 25,000 in the primary on July 24, he will immediately resign as attorney general."

Moody rose to the challenge. Answering Mrs. Ferguson the folowing night in a speech at San Antonio he said, "So eager am I to rid the state of everything they stand for, that I accept the challenge of Jim issued in his wife's name. . . . [This wager] assures the state of a short, quick, and decisive engagement, with a final result on the night of July 24." Moody's friends, perhaps remembering the loyalty of the people to Jim Ferguson, criticized the attorney general for accepting the bet; Moody's reply was that thereby he had done the people of Texas a favor. He said it was a public duty to return the ex-governor to his Bosque County ranch as soon as possible.

Ferguson was delighted that Moody had accepted the challenge. "The governor," Ferguson exulted, "has got the attorney general in the political electric chair, and she is going to electrocute him on July 24."

But Ferguson had guessed wrong. The results of the first Democratic primary showed that Moody had received 409,732 votes; Mrs. Ferguson, 283,482. The four other candidates in the race received sufficient combined votes to make a runoff necessary under the law—unless one of the candidates withdrew. Citizens eagerly awaited some announcement from the governor, for Moody had received substantially more votes than Mrs. Ferguson, but she ignored for two weeks the subject of the wager and her promised resignation. During that time more than two-thirds of the county Democratic conventions passed resolutions asking that she quit the office, and many of the state's newspapers joined in demanding the same thing. The second week in August Mrs. Ferguson finally announced that she would not resign "and turn the state over to the Ku Klux." She declared that she would ask the legislature to pass a law compelling the Ku Klux Klan to register its membership. Replying to Moody's charges of government by proxy and irresponsible government, Mrs. Ferguson said, "Invisible government is a lot worse than irresponsible government."

The runoff was comparatively short and politically quiet. Moody's enormous lead in the July contest had given his friends a feeling that further work was unnecessary, and it apparently convinced Ferguson supporters that their cause was doomed. The August vote therefore was no surprise: Moody, 495,723; Mrs. Ferguson, 270,595.

The conservative government of Texas' first woman chief executive came to an end on January 17, 1927, with the inauguration of Dan Moody. The youthful new governor was progressive, eager to bring about changes, hopeful of retaining efficiency while eliminating waste. And in those areas where he had power, he did quite well; the agencies over which he had full control were quickly overhauled and made to work honestly and productively, and in his appointments Moody maintained a noticeably high standard in selecting his men. With the legislature, however, the new governor did not fare so well.

Moody had not come to office with a definite or insistent legislative program, and like Governor Neff, Moody was more progressive than the lawmakers who convened to work with him. To the Fortieth Legislature the ex-attorney general presented proposals calling for a scientific system of taxation, reforming the judicial system and court procedure, increasing the number of justices on the Supreme Court from three to nine, establishing civil service regulations for the various state departments and a unified system of accounting, and increasing the gasoline tax levy in order to build new and better highways.

The legislators went along with the chief executive in about one half of his recommendations. More money was voted for the public schools and for higher education, the textbook scandal was cleared up, and hundreds of miles of improved highways were approved on the basis of an increase in the gasoline tax to three cents per gallon. But there was no reform in the system of taxation; no changes were made in the cumbersome judicial system or court procedure; no attempts were made to establish a civil service system for state agencies; and no uniform method of accounting was imposed.

Despite his poor legislative record, Governor Moody became a nationally known figure during his first term. He attended the Jackson Day dinner of the national Democratic party held in Washington, D. C., in 1928, and considerable interest was shown in him there. Alfred E. Smith, governor of New York and the probable nominee of the party for the presidency in the coming election, was known to favor a Southerner as a running mate, and many newspapers felt that Moody might be that man. However, late in February Moody announced that he would be a candidate for a second term as governor of Texas.

Then in June 1928 the Democratic national convention met in Houston, and the governor of Texas played a conspicuous role in its proceedings. He headed the state's delegation to the convention, was active on the platform committee, and helped write in a plank declaring that the Volstead Act (a national prohibition law) should be rigidly enforced. Yet the Democratic party nominated Al Smith, an opponent of prohibition, and for this Moody suffered. Texas drys opposed the governor because he supported Smith, while the wets in the state worked against Moody because he had helped write a dry plank into the Democratic platform.

In the race for the Democratic nomination for governor of Texas, Moody was opposed by L. J. Wardlaw, a Fort Worth lawyer known to be a good friend of James Ferguson. Wardlaw had grown up in the West Texas town of Ballinger, was known as a successful businessman, and enjoyed the benefit of never having been in politics. He had the support of the Klan, many prohibitionists and anti-prohibitionists, and the Ferguson following.

Wardlaw made an active campaign, charging Moody with inefficiency and blaming him for his poor legislative record. Wardlaw asserted that the governor had "broken most of his promises to the people," ridiculed Moody's claim to honesty and fairness, and attacked the record of the State Highway Commission for extravagance and favoritism.

Among Moody supporters, however, there was little doubt about the outcome of the primary. Moody himself actively campaigned only during the last two weeks of the race, contenting himself with an account of his two years in office and outlining his plans for a second term.

Election returns from the July primary showed that Moody had received 442,080 votes; Wardlaw, 245,508. The governor had won the nomination without a runoff. The vote was about as everyone had expected; the only real excitement in the race was the contest for a United States Senate seat held by Earle B. Mayfield. After a spirited battle Tom Connally defeated the incumbent.

In the November general election, there was the usual lack of interest in state offices; it was a foregone conclusion that the Democratic nominees would win. But in the race for the presidency, there was no certainty. Al Smith, the Democratic candidate, was a Catholic, a wet, a big-city politician, and seemingly a foreigner. (Smith, a second-generation American, spoke with an accent.) The Republican candidate, Herbert Hoover, was known as a humanitarian, a Protestant, and a great American. After a spirited campaign that involved gossip, smear tactics, and prejudice, Texas for the first time cast its electoral votes for a Republican.

After such a bitter contest, a let-down of interest was to be expected, and the Moody inauguration of January 1929 passed almost unnoticed, lasting only twenty minutes. In his message to the new legislature, the governor made his recommendations, asking primarily for the same reform laws he had requested two years previously. In his relations with the legislature during his second term, Moody received more criticism for the number of bills he vetoed than for the number of laws actually passed. He refused to accept an appropriations bill, the total spending of which exceeded the estimated revenue for the coming biennium, and he vetoed the Party Loyalty Bill and the Red River Validation Bill. After the legislature adjourned, Moody felt it necessary to call five special sessions, but still the record of accomplishments was disappointing. The one major exception was an act providing for the appointment by the governor of a "state auditor and efficiency expert," who was to be clothed with authority to audit all departments of the state government and to recommend uniform methods of keeping the state's accounts.

A problem of long standing, one that politicians constantly used as an issue before the voters, was resolutely faced by Moody—prison reform. In 1929 the state's prison property consisted of the main plant at Huntsville and more than one hundred sections of farmland scattered about the state in several farms. Despite the fact that many prisoners had no training for agricultural work, the managers of the prison system usually took the position that about ninety percent of the 4,500 inmates should be kept at work on the farms. After checking the reports, Moody declared that the prison system was twenty-five years behind the times, was overcrowded, helped spread diseases among the inmates, and had no facilities to reform convicts. He frequently added that the penitentiary at Huntsville was a "firetrap." As a reform he suggested centralization at one location of all the state's prison facilities and increased emphasis on industrialization rather than on agriculture. He declared that two million dollars were needed to clear the system of debt and keep it on a cash basis; he proposed the creation of a board which would be empowered to sell and purchase land as needed in order to centralize the system, preferably at Huntsville.

The legislature at first refused to follow Moody's plan, but later it created a commission to make a study of the prison systems of other states and to make recommendations for revision of the Texas system. The commission made its survey, but it reached no unanimous conclusion as to what would be best for Texas. A majority report from the commission called for a modern plant to be built within ten miles of Austin with manufacturing rather than agriculture as its principal industry. Moody backed this plan, calling a special session of the legislature in the hope that it would be adopted. But instead the legislature accepted the minority plan which provided for improvements in the prison farms that the state already owned and which recommended an appropriation of $575,000 for that purpose. Moody was greatly disappointed at the work of the legislature, and he allowed the bill to become law without his signature.

Moody's first term was probably the most prosperous in the state's history. His second administration was not as successful from an economic point of view; the Great Depression hit in October 1929. However, the effects of it were not felt in Texas until he had passed out of office, and he completed his four years as chief executive without many discordant notes. The next governor would be the one who danced to the tune of hard times.

7

Sterling, Ferguson, and Hard Times

DURING THE TWENTIES there was much talk of "Coolidge Prosperity." Seemingly Americans had discovered the secrets of economics and were using them to banish hunger and want from the land. In a campaign speech in October 1928 Republican presidential candidate Herbert Hoover declared, "Our American experiment in human welfare has yielded a degree of well-being unparalleled in all the world. It has come nearer to the abolition of poverty, to the abolition of fear and want, than humanity has ever reached before."

Just one year later, in October 1929, the boom collapsed. Following almost a decade of high prices, extravagant living, speculation, installment buying, and unusual pros-

[117]

perity, there was a sharp drop in the New York stock market—the so-called "Crash of 1929"—which heralded the beginning of the Great Depression. The decade of plenty had ended, to be followed by a decade of hard times.

Texans, along with other Americans, suffered during the thirties. Prices for oil and cotton fell to unprecedented low levels; many businesses were forced to close completely, and those remaining open were not operating at full capacity; eight percent of the workers of the state, many of them honest and well-intentioned men and women who honestly sought jobs, were unemployed; state income fell off sharply since many citizens could not pay their taxes, but governmental expenditures continued almost as high as ever.

Hardest hit by the problem of unemployment were the uneducated and the racial minorities. A survey of 1933 dealing with those on relief showed that 5.4 percent of the white population was included, while 8.8 percent of the Negroes were destitute. In 1936 of the 154,323 men registered with the United States Employment Service as looking for work, 26,269 were skilled workers, while 53,997 were semi-skilled and 48,366 were unskilled. Clearly the color of a man's skin and the amount of education or job training he had affected his chances of finding employment.

During the early years of the crisis thousands of needy persons were aided by friends and relatives and by local charities, but as the depression continued and increased in intensity such resources were rapidly exhausted. The federal government under Hoover's administration provided some help, but it was insufficient to care for all the unemployed. As a result thousands of individuals, and sometimes families, began to roam about the country.

They used the highways to such an extent that the term "hitch-hiking" came into general use. Some stole rides on freight trains in an effort to move where work could be found. Others, who did not feel like travelling, set up temporary homes in caves, dugouts, piano boxes, or in abandoned buildings, parks, or the river fronts. Shanty towns grew up in the poorer districts of most major cities; these unsightly groupings were sometimes referred to as "Hoover Heights" or "Hoovervilles," so called because for many months after the start of the hard times the President refused to recognize or admit the existence of a depression, declaring that recovery and prosperity were just around the corner. Many citizens demanded that the President should inform the public as to "which corner of which block in what city." Jackrabbits, eaten by many hungry Texans, were known as "Hoover hogs"; those people sleeping on park benches under newspapers called their covering "Hoover blankets." The public needed a scapegoat for their difficulties, and President Hoover received the blame.

As the depression grew worse, there were many unusual efforts to relieve the suffering and distress. "Send a dime" chain letters were tried in Texas and other states; many Texans were enchanted with Huey Long's promise that he could provide every family in the United States a five-thousand-dollar-a-year income or with Charles Townsend's scheme to give each person over sixty-five two hundred dollars every month. Most Texans, along with the majority of the residents of other states, however, turned to the federal government to cure the ill that had beset the nation. Herbert Hoover was soundly defeated in the election of 1932, and Franklin D. Roosevelt was sent to Washington to give the country a "New Deal." Beginning in 1933 a plethora of legislation was passed, bureaus were created, and money was appropriated—all with the intent of ending the depression.

The Civilian Conservation Corps, the Federal Emergency Relief Administration, the National Youth Administration, the Works Progress Administration, and many other agencies were established to provide direct or indirect relief to people without funds or jobs. In addition, the Agricultural Adjustment Administration, the Federal Deposit Insurance Comporation, the National Recovery Administration, and other agencies attempted in their own way to bring about recovery and stimulate economic development.

Despite all this activity in Washington, despite the ringing debates and editorials about the wisdom of big government and creeping socialism, it was the state governments that bore the heaviest load in fighting the hard times of the thirties, for most of the federal money was expended through state agencies; most of the direct contacts with private individuals were made by state officials, and most of the blame for failures fell on state politicians.

In Texas the first gubernatorial election following the onset of the hard times brought out a few new politicians and a few new ideas, but one of the leading contenders was none other than Miriam Ferguson who campaigned with the usual Ferguson charges and promises. In 1930 her husband made another bid to have his name put on the ballot, but the state Supreme Court refused to issue such an order to the Democratic State Executive Committee. Therefore once again Mrs. Ferguson stepped forward as the Ferguson standard bearer.

Opposing her was a field of ten other candidates, chief among whom were Ross Sterling and Earle B. Mayfield.

Sterling of Houston was chairman of the State Highway Commission during Moody's administration; a banker, oil operator, and railroad owner, he was one of the founders of Humble Oil Company and widely known as a successful businessman. A fellow Houstonian estimated that Sterling was worth "over fifty million dollars," and from the day he announced for the office of governor, he attracted much attention. Earle B. Mayfield of Bosque County had been in the United States Senate from 1923 to 1929, elected as a Klan candidate in 1922 over James Ferguson. Frank Putnam of Houston, himself a candidate for governor in 1930, said that Mayfield was "dry in principle but not in practice" and noted that Mayfield "uses the radio a lot lately—must have struck oil."

Other serious contenders in 1930 included Thomas B. Love, a state senator from Dallas and a veteran prohibitionist; Barry Miller of Dallas, a party regular and a political foe of Love who in 1930 was serving his third term as lieutenant governor; Clint C. Small of Wellington, a state senator and favorite of the independent oil operators; and James Young, a native of East Texas who had served from 1911 to 1921 as a congressman and was known as a vigorous prohibitionist.

Governor Moody thought seriously of entering the race for a third term when at first it appeared the two serious candidates were Mrs. Ferguson and ex-Senator Mayfield. "The prospect of being forced to choose between Earle B. Mayfield and James E. Ferguson is not an inviting one to the people of Texas," the governor declared, adding that neither was "fit for public trust in this state." However, he needed to enter the practice of law and make sufficient money to pay his debts, and he knew that his friend, Ross Sterling, was considering running. Therefore, Moody refused to allow his name to appear on the ballot, even after supporters from Tyler filed a petition on his behalf and paid the one-hundred-dollar filing fee.

Campaigning in 1930 got off to a slow start because of uncertainty about who would be the candidates. Not until June did James Ferguson lose his bid to get his own name on the ballot, and Senator Love, who had led the Hoover Republicans in Texas in 1928, had to appeal to the Democratic executive committee before his name was certified for the Democratic primary. Once the campaigning did get underway, however, it quickly made up for lost ground, generating as much sound and fury as most Texas gubernatorial contests.

Sterling drew more newspaper support than any other candidate. The Houston *Post-Dispatch,* of which he was part owner, editorialized in his behalf, as did the Austin *American,* Dallas *News,* and Houston *Chronicle.* A man of great physical bulk, Sterling was introduced to one audience with the comment, "Now here's your fat boy from Houston!" He was no orator and realized the fact, modestly telling his audiences that they need not expect any flowery speeches from him; instead he spoke in simple language of his own career and his plans for the state government should the people elect him. The plank in his platform that drew the greatest interest and criticism was a call for a bond issue of $300,000,000 to $350,000,000 for the purpose of building state highways. In his opening speech at Huntsville on June 20 before more than five thousand people, Sterling explained his road bond proposal and called for prison reform, better labor conditions, more generous support of education, aid for the farmer and stockman, rigid enforcement of the laws, and an end to factional strife in the state government. He advocated increasing the taxes on sulfur and natural gas and retaining the prevailing tax on oil, but said he would fight any movement to legalize racetrack gambling in Texas, despite the revenue it would raise.

Other candidates ridiculed the road bond proposal. James Young demanded that Sterling resign from the highway commission and forecast that the Houston millionaire would soon "abandon his own child." Ex-Senator Mayfield declared that he was opposed to the bond issue and concentrated his attack on Sterling's great wealth, insisting that as head of Humble Oil and Refining Company, Sterling had "brought Standard Oil into Texas" and was spending an unheard of amount on his campaign.

James Ferguson, who as usual was doing most of the campaigning for his wife, at first ignored the Sterling candidacy, but by July he was concentrating his efforts exclusively against the highway commissioner. At Brenham he said that Sterling was a former Klansman and that his bond issue, if adopted, would increase taxes and the bonded indebtedness of the counties. In a rally at Houston, Ferguson promised that his wife would save the people of Texas seven million dollars a year by eliminating duplication of work in the government, especially by combining the offices of tax assessor and tax collector, and by providing for quarterly tax payments. Irritated by criticism of the Ferguson pardon record, Ferguson not only defended such action but said his wife would "pardon two thousand more" as soon as she took office again.

Sterling, surprised at the volume of criticism of his road bond proposal, answered in July at Coleman. Calling his idea the "Sterling un-bonding plan," he said:

> Instead of saddling a mortgage on the people, I want to do just the opposite. The people and their descendants already have the mortgage in the form of over $200,-000,000 of county road bonds which have driven many of them to the point of bankruptcy.

I want to lift the greater part of the burden the counties have shouldered to help build state highways, and place it on the traffic where it belongs, through a state bond issue based upon the state gasoline tax, so that those who use the highways will pay for them. I want to return to the counties the $75,000,000 to $100,000,000 they have already contributed to state highways.

He remarked that thirty-three states had already adopted the state bond plan and were finding it successful, but added that if the legislators could find a better plan to build good roads, one that would take the road tax burden from farmers and home owners, he would be glad to support it.

As election day approached, every major candidate was ascribed a place in the runoff by his friends and supporters. However, only two candidates could make it, and those two were Mrs. Ferguson and Sterling. The vote was Mrs. Ferguson, 242,959; Sterling, 170,754; Small, 138,934; Love, 87,068; Young, 73,385; Miller, 54,652; and Mayfield, 54,459.

The political turmoil quieted during the first half of August as the two remaining candidates prepared for the runoff and the public speculated about the attitudes of the five defeated aspirants. Senator Small at first declined to indicate his preference, but after ten days announced that he would vote for Sterling. Senator Love and former Congressman Young said they also would support the Houston millionaire, while Mayfield and Miller urged the election of Mrs. Ferguson. About the same time Governor Moody, who had made no speeches during the July race, came out for Sterling, stating that he would support any candidate who opposed the Fergusons.

The issues faded into the background as the runoff neared, and a discussion of personalities became the prime topic at campaign rallies. Mike Hogg, a South Texas Sterling supporter, declared, "The plain people make a great mistake if they think Ferguson has changed. Everybody knows his record." In Waco on August 7, Governor Moody said that Ferguson's claim to helping the farmer was "bunk," that Ferguson's statement that he was a friend of the laboring man was "a farce." Sterling, speaking at Hillsboro the following day, answered a Ferguson charge that he was ignorant of governmental affairs by stating, "I know enough to tell the state's money and my money apart."

At last came the day of the election. Texans selected the Democratic nominee and, as usual, their next governor. The final totals showed that Sterling had received 473,371 votes, Mrs. Ferguson 384,402. Sterling carried 150 of the 250 counties reporting returns.

When Sterling took office in January 1931, his immediate problem was the Great Depression which was making its full effects felt. Sterling felt it to be his duty to cut state expenditures to a minimum and therefore became known for his many vetoes of appropriations. In his message to the legislature he made the usual recommendations, especially commending to the lawmakers the platform of the Democratic party. There was no lack of harmony between the governor and the legislature, since Sterling made no real demands for action. Little was done to relieve the state's financial emergency in a "do-nothing session," although the Forty-second Legislature met for 131 days. The sulfur tax was raised from 55 cents to 75 cents a ton, and a levy of five cents a barrel was placed on cement. A cigarette tax of three cents a package was authorized, along with a two percent tax on natural gas.

A state income tax bill failed to pass, as did the redistricting bill, a tax equalization act, and a cotton control plan. The final appropriations bill emerging from the regular session greatly exceeded expected revenues, and Sterling felt compelled to veto almost three million dollars from it, cutting new buildings voted for state colleges and the University of Texas and money for the summer schools of 1933.

Ironically, the greatest problem facing Governor Sterling during his term as chief executive, coming during an era of hard times and want, was one of overproduction. There was too much oil being produced in the state. Even before Sterling moved into the governor's mansion, the state's oil production was so great that prices were falling. Some of the wells in the Yates Field in West Texas were so productive that they alarmed the entire oil industry; one well alone flowed at a rate of 127,600 barrels a day. Then, approximately one month before Sterling was elected governor, the first well in the East Texas oil field was brought in. By the end of Sterling's term, just two years later, more than ten thousand producing wells had been drilled in East Texas. The pioneer in this field was Columbus Marion ("Dad") Joiner, a wildcatter who moved to Texas in 1927 and secured several leases in Rusk County and vicinity. The first two wells he drilled were dry holes, but still he persisted, selling stock in his venture to anyone who would buy to finance a third effort. At a depth of 3,700 feet Joiner was ready to abandon the project when suddenly his driller declared he saw oil in the drilling mud. A few days later the well began flowing, and another boom began, one as great as any that had preceded it. Added to the tremendous output of the other producing fields, the volume of oil flowing from Texas wells threatened to ruin the petroleum industry. Oil, the chief source of Sterling's business success as a private citizen, became his most troublesome problem as a public official.

As the price of oil tumbled lower and lower, finally reaching eight cents a barrel, the governor called three special sessions of the legislature to seek a solution. When efforts to allow the railroad commission to enforce production restrictions failed to become law, Sterling on August 17, 1931, ordered national guard troops into the East Texas field and declared martial law. For a short time thereafter, the field was completely shut down. The legislature thereupon voted into effect a law empowering the railroad commission to set production allowables, and proration (as this power was termed) was put into effect. Six months later, a federal court ruled that Governor Sterling had acted without authority in declaring martial law, and the national guardsmen were removed.

During the six months that martial law was in effect in the East Texas field, the oil producers protested loudly against the governor's actions, but thereby a great deal of waste was prevented. Thereafter, with the railroad commission regulating the petroleum industry in Texas, production of illegal oil gradually declined. Stabilization was promoted as state and federal laws were strengthened, the courts stiffened in their attitudes, and the proration plan was upheld by the courts.

In addition to the troubles brought about by the overproduction of oil, the low price of cotton caused difficulties for the Sterling administration. Late in the summer of 1931 farmers were receiving five and one-half cents a pound for middle basis cotton. Sterling recommended and the legislature, in special session, passed a bill on September 22 reducing cotton acreage in the state by fifty percent for the coming year. But the act was held unconstitutional by the courts in February 1932 because of the "inherent and constitutional right of the citizen to use his property as he chooses." Prices continued to drop, reaching a thirty-three-year low on June 1, 1932, of 5.05 cents a pound, causing the farmers' distress to increase correspondingly. Since about half the Texas voters were tenant farmers whose major crop was cotton, the cotton problem brought even more hardship to the state than did the ruinous price of crude oil.

Sterling's road bond proposal, the one that had caused him such difficulties as a candidate, was never submitted to the voters by the legislature, nor was it enacted into law. Instead the lawmakers in a called session in September 1932 disregarded Sterling's proposal and passed a substitute measure setting aside one fourth of the revenue from the gasoline tax to be used to reimburse the counties for the money they had spent to build roads that had subsequently become part of the state highway system.

James Ferguson, who had been keeping a watchful eye on the Sterling administration and who was well aware of the financial misery caused by the hard times and low prices, concluded that 1932 would be a good "Ferguson year." Therefore Mrs. Ferguson announced for governor in mid-February on a platform of lower taxes. At first her announcement drew little attention, but early in the summer her bandwagon picked up speed and followers, causing increasing comment about the possibility of another Ferguson administration. The editor of the *Texas Weekly* declared that the real issue in the contest was "responsible government," adding that "Every citizen knows that in case of her success Jim will be the real governor." Three weeks later the far-away New York *Evening Post* carried the statement, "If the majority of the voters in the Democratic primary see as clearly as the

Texas Weekly, the Lone Star State will be spared the misfortune of another Ferguson administration." A leading Philadelphia newspaper editorialized, "It is hardly imaginable that the people of Texas will again be gripped by the old insanity that put "Ma" Ferguson in the governor's chair."

Because Governor Sterling did not announce for reelection until late in the spring, several well-known Texans, including former Governor Moody and Lieutenant Governor Edgar Witt of Waco, considered seeking the post. Sterling's announcement on May 14, however, caused all except Tom Hunter, a wealthy independent oil operator from Wichita Falls, to withdraw, leaving a three-way race for the governorship.

The Fergusons, as usual, had opened their campaign in Waco, and three weeks later Governor Sterling conducted his first rally in the same city. Speaking in general about responsible government, he insisted that the deficit that had been forecast for the fiscal year had been overcome. He reviewed his two years in office and presented his platform: economy, abolition of the fee system at all levels of government, conservation of natural resources, and promotion of home ownership. Warming to his task, the governor spoke at Brenham about his opponent. "A man is running for governor behind his wife's skirts who wants to take the highway fund and divide it into $10,000,000 to the general fund, $10,000,000 to the school fund, and $10,000,000 to Jim's fund," he declared, answering a Ferguson call to divert money from the highway fund to the general revenue fund and the school. Answering critics of his handling of the crisis in the oil fields, he said, "I have no apology to make for [declaring] martial law in East Texas. It saved the state $6,000,000 in taxes, and it saved the people of Texas $40,000,000 in the value of their products." He asserted that his handling of the situation had increased the price of oil from ten cents to one dollar a barrel and had stabilized the business of the independent oil men of Texas.

During the last two weeks of the campaign numerous well-known speakers came to the aid of Sterling. Dan Moody at Cleburne spoke at length on the menace of proxy government and declared that while Mrs. Ferguson was governor her husband had an income of $148,000, "a most phenomenal record for an unemployed man. . . ."

Meanwhile Ferguson was busy chipping away at the Sterling record. In a speech at Brenham, Ferguson said that the state treasury would have a deficit of $6,500,000 by August. In Houston he accused the highway commission of "autocracy, incompetency, and waste." He asserted that Governor Sterling had two thousand men on highway jobs for political purposes, men who would not have jobs "thirty days after the election." He renewed his attacks on the highway commission at Cuero and Yorktown, adding a new charge that there was a shortage of over $100,-000,000 in the highway fund for the last five and one-half years. He called Sterling a "fat head" and referred to him as the "present vacancy" and the "present encumbrance."

The state auditor declared on July 20 that the highway fund was in perfect order; but Ferguson kept repeating his charges of a huge shortage, and undoubtedly many people believed him.

Election time arrived at last, a warm, clear summer day that saw an unusually large turnout because a national prohibition referendum was on the Democratic primary ticket. The vote was Mrs. Ferguson, 402,238; Sterling, 296,383; and Hunter, 220,391. Mrs. Ferguson carried two thirds of the counties, running generally ahead in every section of the state. For the runoff campaign of

1932, just as two years previously, it was to be a Ferguson-Sterling struggle.

There was little new in the form of issues, charges, claims, or procedures in the August campaign. During the five weeks between the primary and the runoff, the Fergusons waged a week-end fight, grouping their rallies to fall in the period from Thursday to Saturday and resting and making plans during the rest of the time. Ferguson kept repeating the charge of a $100,000,000 shortage in the highway fund and said that Sterling was "attempting to buy his way into the governor's office again." He predicted that his wife would win easily, and added, "I'll be in there picking up chips and bringing in water for Mamma."

Despite the discouragement of many of his followers because of the Ferguson lead of more than one hundred thousand votes in the primary, Sterling made a very aggressive and complete campaign through the month of August, giving eight to ten speeches a day which were climaxed by a nightly rally at some large city or county seat. He professed optimism at his chances of reelection, pointing to the 1930 runoff which Mrs. Ferguson lost after getting forty-five percent of the votes in the primary. He felt that history would repeat itself, but some of his friends saw the handwriting on the wall. Colonel Sam Robertson of San Benito asked the governor to withdraw in favor of Tom Hunter, declaring in a telegram, "You are an in. You cannot win in such a time as this. Thomas Jefferson, George Washington, or Abe Lincoln, if in office today, could not be reelected. The voters of 1932 are as rational as the mob who crucified Christ."

About the middle of August came interesting news; in 132 counties, mostly in the Ferguson strongholds of East Texas, there had been 359,667 poll tax receipts issued in

1932, but 397,386 votes had been cast in the July primary. Of these counties, one had a tie vote, Sterling had carried seventeen, Hunter twenty, and the Fergusons ninety-four.

Despite the cries of fraud and "ballot box stuffing," the runoff was held on schedule. The results were Ferguson, 477,644; Sterling, 473,846. By less than four thousand votes out of almost a million cast, Mrs. Ferguson had once again received the coveted Democratic nomination for governor. Still the Sterling forces were not willing to give up without a fight. Pointing to about one hundred counties where more votes had been cast in the runoff than there were poll tax receipts issued, the governor and his friends made every effort to get a recount, but to no avail. The legislature, in a fourth called session, debated at length the need of a legislative investigation, but the proposal was killed just before the Democratic state convention convened in Lubbock on September 17. The convention certified Mrs. Ferguson as the party's nominee and recommended her platform to the voters and to the legislature. Sterling at last had to concede defeat; it would seem that Sterling, like President Hoover, who lost to Franklin D. Roosevelt that year, was a political victim of the widespread discontent with the prevailing hard times.

Perhaps the Fergusons were mellowing with age; at least, Mrs. Ferguson's second administration was an economical one and met with less criticism than did her first one. Inaugurated on January 17, 1933, she called upon the legislature for harmony and cooperation in dealing with the woeful financial condition of the state. Her solution to the deficit and the need for more revenue was a three percent sales tax, which she estimated would raise forty-five million dollars annually, and a cut of fifteen million dollars in the budget for the next biennium.

The sales tax proposal raised many voices to full volume, some for and some against. Peter Molyneaux, editor of the *Texas Weekly*, called it "plain common sense," and the tax was supported by a majority of Texas newspapers, including the Houston *Post* and Houston *Chronicle*. An editorial in the *Chronicle*, however, declared, "The proposed three percent sales tax, as advocated by the governor, would tax everything from diaper pins to pine coffins if enacted into law, and would cause more hell-raising in Texas than we care to be mixed up in." The Bartlett *Times* likewise indicated its disapproval: "The Texas Legislature, with the wisdom of donkeys, seriously contemplates passing a three percent sales tax. . . ."

Actually the editor of the Bartlett *Times* was oversimplifying the attitude of the lawmakers, for a press survey showed that House members preferred an income tax; the Senate seemed disposed to give the governor what she wanted.

Early in March the House Committee on Revenue and Taxation reported favorably on a bill that combined a sales tax and an income tax, with the latter predominating. The proposed act, by a vote of nine to nothing, died in the Senate Finance Committee. The governor thereupon asked the state comptroller and the state auditor to prepare a statement about the financial condition of the treasury; this statement she sent to the legislature, calling upon the lawmakers to raise revenue "in any way you see fit" in order to end the deficit of more than eighteen million dollars that was forecast for August 31, 1933.

Still the legislators took no action. Mrs. Ferguson a few days later proposed an income tax on the gross earnings of corporations, one that would bring in some twenty-five million dollars a year. She declared that such a measure would "go a long way toward balancing our budget," but apparently the legislature did not care for the proposal. The only revenue-raising measure it passed was one increasing the tax on oil to two cents a barrel; it was estimated that this tax would bring in an additional eight million dollars a year. And the lawmakers did cut thirteen millions from the biennial appropriation.

Another important measure passed by the 1933 session dealt with the Depression. Governor Ferguson persuaded the lawmakers to pass and send to the voters a constitutional amendment providing for the issuance of twenty million dollars in relief bonds. That same year, by a vote of more than two to one, Texans approved the measure, and Mrs. Ferguson called a special session of the legislature to implement the program. A special administrative agency, known as the Texas Rehabilitation and Relief Commission, was created to oversee the spending of state and federal funds for employment, rehabilitation, and relief. The law provided that the governor should preside over the meetings of this commission. In actuality Mrs. Ferguson never attended the sessions of the commission, allowing her husband to sit in her place instead. The relief bonds were sold at a premium, and the funds helped in many ways to relieve the misery and suffering of numerous Texas families.

Other than this important measure, the Forty-third Legislature accomplished very little although it met for a record 143 days. The state was redistricted for congressional purposes; horse race gambling and prize fighting were made legal; per capita patterns of appropriations for state educational institutions were begun; and the legislature provided for a referendum on the question of legalizing the manufacture and sale of 3.2 percent beer and the repeal of the Eighteenth Amendment (prohibition).

And it was the Forty-third Legislature that received the Graves-Woodruff Reorganization Bill, perhaps better known as the Griffinhagen Report. In the previous session of the legislature, during the administration of Sterling, a joint committee consisting of five members was created and authorized to investigate all state departments, institutions, and the judiciary. On the committee were Senators Grady Woodruff and Carl Hardin and Representatives Harry N. Graves, Phil L. Sanders, and J. T. Terrell. They employed a private firm, Griffinhagen and Associates, to make surveys and act as consultants. The committee worked for almost two years, checking into every facet and phase of the state government and its administration, and prepared a comprehensive report totalling forty thousand words. This report recommended the reorganization and consolidation of 129 existing state bureaus and commissions into twenty new ones, which would save the state about $1,500,000 annually, and a reorganization of the state colleges, which would save $2,000,000 to $4,000,000 per year.

Naturally such proposed changes brought a great deal of discussion. The far-away New York *Times*, in a long article on the report, perhaps best summarized the debate: "There are no radical suggestions, no seemingly impossible proposals, nothing that does not appear wholly practical. . . . The plan is designed to save at least $6,000,000 annually . . . but it is thought that the proposals will be generally discarded."

Shortly after the Forty-third Legislature convened, the Griffinhagen Report was made available to the lawmakers. Almost immediately a bill was introduced in the House for reorganization of the institutions of higher learning.

The measure created a wave of protest. Briefly it provided for the consolidation of the two colleges at Denton, the abandonment of Southwest Texas State Teachers College owing to its proximity to the University of Texas at Austin, and abandoning or turning into junior colleges the teachers colleges at Nacogdoches, Alpine, Canyon, and Commerce. The bill was sent to the Committee on Education and reported favorably, but it got no further.

Two proposed laws were introduced to reorganize the executive departments of the state government. The Woodruff Bill passed the Senate and was sent to the House, but it was loaded with amendments that defeated its purpose. The Graves Bill was introduced in the House for the same purpose, passed by a vote of 105 to 22, and was sent to the Senate; there by a vote of 17 to 9 it was "Recommitted to the State Affairs Committee."

In effect, then, the proposals contained in the Griffinhagen Report were "generally discarded," just as the New York *Times* had predicted.

Shortly after the legislature adjourned, the referendum on repeal of the Eighteenth Amendment was submitted to the voters of the state. On August 26, 1933, Texans at the polls indicated by a ratio of three to two that they favored abandoning the "Noble Experiment," as Herbert Hoover termed the ascendency of the prohibitionists. Beer sales were legalized in the state by a vote of two to one. Texans followed the national trend in this election, for twenty states had already acted favorably on the repeal amendment; none had defeated it.

During the remainder of her term, following the adjournment of the legislature, Mrs. Ferguson did little to cause controversy. She did continue her "open door" policy in granting pardons, causing some complaints, but in general she showed that she had learned a great deal about managing the state in a quiet manner. Actually Texans were not particularly concerned with events at the state capital, busy as they were discussing the actions and efforts of Franklin D. Roosevelt and the New Deal in Washington, D. C. The new President was trying many experiments to end the Great Depression and restore prosperity. More and more Texans, along with the residents of other states, were made to feel that all really important governmental action occurred at the federal level.

But still the economic indicators of the country spiraled downward, and the hard times continued.

8

A Political Interlude

In an article about the Texas Democratic primary of 1934, the New York *Times* described the voters of the Lone Star State as "apathetic" and called the contest "the quietest in more than twenty years." And the *Times* was correct, for Texans that year paid little attention to politics.

The 1934 contest came in the middle of a decade of hard times, a period during which Texans were more concerned with keeping food on their tables and roofs over their heads than with events remote from the immediacy of hunger and unemployment. The state was in the clutches of a severe drouth; thousands were still on relief; delinquent taxes were piling up; the state debt was increasing, and farm prices were agonizingly low. Yet none of the reforms of the federal or state government had brought an end to the depression, and Texans in 1934 paid little heed to politics. The summer of 1934 marked the start of a four-year interlude, a quiet backwater, in the roar and spectacle, the carnival atmosphere that had been Texas politics during the preceding two decades. Sandwiched between the administrations of two colorful and controversial governors, Miriam Ferguson and W. Lee O'Daniel, these four years stand as a time of relative harmony between the chief executive and the legislature, relative agreement about the major problems of the state, very little scandal, and a temporary eclipse of the Fergusons. Some experts have labelled this period "a new era in Texas politics," but in actuality it was a return to the pre-Ferguson age when reforms were quietly accomplished, when politics were conducted on a dignified level, and when relative peace reigned in Austin.

The three leading candidates for governor in 1934 were James V. Allred, Tom Hunter, and C. C. McDonald, all of Wichita Falls. Minor candidates who paid the filing fee and had their names included on the ballot were Edgar Witt of Waco, Clint Small who had moved from Wellington to Amarillo, and Maury Hughes of Dallas. So strong was the two-term tradition in Texas politics that Mrs. Ferguson did not announce for reelection.

All six of the aspirants were able men, experienced in government, but none of them was well known on a state-wide basis. Allred, after serving in the United States navy in World War I, practiced law in Wichita Falls; in 1923 Governor Pat Neff had appointed him district attorney of the 30th Judicial District. Defeated for attorney general by a narrow margin in 1926, Allred waited four years and was elected to the post in 1930. He attracted wide attention by his persistent fight against monopolies and his attempts to enforce the antitrust laws, and in 1932 he was reelected without a runoff. His platform in 1934 included the creation of a Commission on Public Utilities, a referendum on repeal of the state constitutional prohibition amendment, a decrease in taxes, a graduated chain store tax, the creation of a modern state police force patterned after the Federal Bureau of Investigation, and stronger control of lobbyists.

Tom Hunter and Clint Small had both appeared in preceding gubernatorial campaigns. Hunter in 1934 announced that he favored a reduction of state taxes, liberal support to education, state regulation of public utilities, an increase in the tax on sulfur, and enactment of the reforms in the Griffinhagen Report. He widely discussed a fund-raising program which he labelled a "blended tax plan" and included a "net earnings tax" for both individuals and corporations in the upper income brackets. Small's platform was almost identical.

Charles C. McDonald, although a newcomer to politics in his own behalf, had wide experience in campaigning for others. He helped Colquitt in 1910, for which he was appointed secretary of state, and he aided the Fergusons in their many races. It was generally understood that McDonald was the Ferguson candidate for governor in 1934, and Ferguson did endorse the Wichita Falls teacher and lawyer. McDonald promised if elected to work for a shorter work day and week in order to provide employment for many additional people, to defend organized labor's right to bargain collectively, to help every family own its own home, to oppose prohibition, and to abolish the ad valorem tax on real estate and personal property.

All the candidates called for old age pensions; all favored economy, education, and better state services of all kinds at low cost; and all except McDonald spoke about the excessive number of pardons that had been granted and declared themselves in favor of a change in the system to provide a pardons and parole board. In fact, so similar were the platforms of the various candidates that there were many charges and counter-charges of stealing "issues."

The Allred campaign had variety, entertainment, and originality. A writer for the Houston *Post* said the thirty-five-year-old attorney general had talent as an evangelist and an actor, along with expert oratorical and political ability. Allred made the pardoning power and control of the lobbyists the main issues of his campaign, speaking in all sections of the state. Soon he became the chief target of all the other candidates, and newspaper polls showed him to be the favorite to lead in the primary.

Ferguson made speeches for McDonald and predicted that Allred and McDonald would be the contestants in the runoff. There were those, however, who declared that Ferguson's support actually hurt McDonald's chances, for since there were so few issues dividing the candidates the race narrowed down to personalities, with pro- and anti-Ferguson sentiment playing a prominent role. And the Ferguson critics were right, for the primary results showed that Allred had secured 298,903 votes; Hunter, 243,254; McDonald, 207,200; Small, 125,324; Witt, 62,376; and Hughes, 58,815. It was to be an Allred-Hunter contest.

The runoff campaign began only a few days after the results of the July primary were known. Hunter and Allred swung back to the race with unusual energy and enthusiasm, pursuing votes in all parts of the state. Since Allred had been the favorite in the primary, most of the defeated candidates decided to aid Hunter in the runoff. Even James Ferguson, who had fought both candidates bitterly in the July contest, soon announced that he would support Hunter. Ross Sterling endorsed Allred and his program.

During the runoff contest, the issues were debated at length, but the campaign actually was personal and bitter. Hunter declared that Allred had no platform and no plan for taxation. He asserted that the suits against the oil trust for seventeen million dollars, brought by Allred as attorney general, were for political purposes only, not for any violation of state laws.

Allred was equally sharp-tongued. He ridiculed the Hunter proposal to combine over one hundred state bureaus under the leadership of five men, calling it "Uncle Tom's Cabinet" and declaring that such a plan was dangerous, for if carried out it would lead to a centralization of power and perhaps even a dictatorship. He produced letters written by Hunter to the House Committee on Revenue and Taxation urging the levy of a sales tax, and he insisted that Hunter's "blended tax" was nothing but the same thing in a different form.

As the campaign drew to a close, Hunter forecast his own victory by a majority of 200,000, while Allred contented himself by predicting his own election by a majority of 100,000. The returns showed that Allred was the better prophet, for he secured 499,343 votes to Hunter's 459,106.

Political experts immediately declared that the Fergusons, whose candidates had been defeated in both the primary and the runoff, were finished in Texas. The New York *Times* carried an article that spoke of the "voluntary retirement of one of the most dominant and, at the same time, most turbulent families in Texas political history." But Peter Molyneaux, editor of the *Texas Weekly* and an astute observer of the Texas scene, was more cautious. "Whether this is the final exit of the Fergusons it would require a hardy order of prophecy to say," he wrote, reminding his readers that on four previous occasions the Fergusons had been "eliminated," yet each time had staged a come-back.

Once he became chief executive, Allred recognized that relief and taxation were the two chief problems of the time. In his recommendations to the Forty-fourth Legislature, he called for the lawmakers to work closely with the general plan of President Franklin D. Roosevelt for helping the unemployed. He asked for permission to issue the remaining $3,500,000 of the $20,000,000 in bonds that Texans had voted for relief in 1932, expressing the opinion that the federal government might vote to match state funds for old age pensions that were "just, humane, and inevitable." He called for the legislators to establish a planning board to work in harmony with the planned federal program of relief. In matters of taxation he asked for a chain store tax, an abolition of the ad valorem tax, economy in government, and an attempt to remedy the "tremendous deficit" in the state treasury.

In other fields he turned his attention on the lobbyists, calling for regulation of the plague of representatives of pressure groups that descended on Austin at each session of the legislature. He asked that the legislators authorize a separate conservation commission to regulate the production of gas and oil, that they generously support primary and higher education, that they increase the powers of the board of pardons and parole, that they repeal legalized racetrack gambling (which had been authorized during the Ferguson administration), and that they institute a measure to repeal constitutional prohibition.

Early in the spring, it became more and more apparent

that the financial problems of the state were growing. Allred did not hesitate to suggest solutions, calling for taxes on gasoline to be used outside the state, an increase in the tax on natural gas, increases in the levies on sulfur, pipelines, and inheritances, and a selective sales tax on luxuries. He even went so far as to declare that an income tax would be "one of the fairest solutions of the problem the state could make."

As usual the legislators listened to the governor's proposals, and then as usual they did as they liked. Sitting for 125 days, the lawmakers considered 1,620 bills, including 80 proposed constitutional amendments, a record number. The thirteen amendments subsequently sent to the voters for ratification or rejection included such proposals as the repeal of statewide prohibition, establishment of a system of old age pensions, abolition of the fee system, and change in the system of suspended sentences. Education was dealt with liberally; the institutions of higher learning received an appropriation of eleven million dollars, and rural aid measures totalled ten million. The legislature voted to follow Allred's recommendation for a unified state police force by establishing the Department of Public Safety, an amalgamation of the famed Texas Rangers with the Highway Patrol. A state planning board was authorized, and the remaining relief bonds voted by the people were ordered issued.

The beer tax amendment, chain store tax bills, natural resource tax bills, and other items on the governor's list of revenue-raising measures to balance the budget all died, as did the repeal of racetrack gambling. One North Texas newspaper editorial stated, "*Sine die* adjournment of the Texas Legislature Saturday concluded a session running very true to form of recent years in the amount of necessary legislation left pending and compelling a special session." On all sides it was freely predicted that a special session would have to be called in September to raise revenue and, it was hoped by reformers, pass a law prohibiting racetrack gambling.

In the August special election on the constitutional amendments, five were accepted by the voters, including repeal of statewide prohibition and authorization of an old-age pension system. Governor Allred thereupon called the lawmakers back to Austin for a special session on September 16 to implement the pension plan; after a thirty-day session the legislature adjourned after having done nothing except pass a chain store tax bill which many lawmakers thought was unsatisfactory and unconstitutional. A second called session subsequently met, passed a new drivers' license bill, set up an old age pension plan, and established a liquor control board to supervise the alcoholic beverage trade. Under the scale of taxes on liquor that was established, it was hoped that the state would profit by ten thousand dollars a day. Dealers were to be licensed, local options were authorized, and the sale of liquor by the drink was prohibited.

Despite this work, the major issues of the 1934 campaign were still unsolved, and these became the basis of the 1936 contest. The outstanding question was the problem of financing the old age pensions, an enormously expensive proposition.

Besides Allred, who announced his candidacy for re-election early, there were four other aspirants to the chief executive's position. Tom Hunter was making a third effort; newcomers included F. W. Fischer of Tyler, Roy Sanderford of Belton, and Pierce P. Brooks of Dallas.

As governor, Allred had generally pleased the people and the press during his first term. The legislature had failed to carry out all his recommendations, especially in connection with raising taxes, but Allred had persuaded the lawmakers to enact a considerable part of the Democratic platform of 1934. During his first two years in office, he had received the fullest recognition from the Roosevelt administration in Washington and had been named by the Junior Chamber of Commerce of the United States as the "Outstanding Young Man of America" in 1935. At the Democratic national convention in 1936, it was Allred who had renominated Vice-President John Nance Garner of Texas for reelection as Roosevelt's running mate. During June, a month before the primary and a time when the other candidates were busy seeking votes, the governor helped open the Texas Centennial celebration in Dallas. He also entertained Roosevelt and his family when the President visited the state for the Centennial celebration. These duties took up so much of Allred's time during June that it was obvious that he would not find time to make a long campaign.

About July 1 Allred earnestly started his bid for reelection, opening his verbal guns at Waxahachie. He declared that Texas was virtually out of the depression and that the state's financial condition would constantly improve. "The deficit will be entirely wiped out within two years without additional taxes," he assured his listeners. He asserted that during his administration more laws favorable to labor had been passed than under any other governor and that twenty-four of the thirty-one planks of the Democratic platform had been enacted in full or in part, an excellent record in Texas politics. In reply to the general criticism of the pension plan that had become law, he said, speaking at Brady, that only the legislators could make changes in it.

During his first eighteen months in office, Allred had been so much in demand to speak at dedication ceremonies that his opponents in the 1936 contest criticized him for his "ribbon cutting" activities. So numerous were the references to this normal function of a governor that Allred finally complimented his opponents for having given the people a new issue in Texas politics, that of "ribbon cutting."

In his last week of campaigning Allred took notice of another of his opponents' constant criticisms—that the old-age pension plan enacted by the Forty-fourth Legislature was financed only by income from the liquor business. The governor answered that he had not recommended taxing liquor to support the state's aged population, but since the voters of Texas had decided to allow the state to regulate liquor sales he personally felt that alcoholic beverages should be taxed. He declared that a look at the record would show that in 1935 he had suggested to the legislature that "oil, gas, sulfur, inheritances, franchises, pipelines, luxuries, and chain stores" should be taxed. He castigated his opponents for their extravagant promises to aid all the elderly citizens, asserting that if all citizens over sixty-five were paid pensions it would cost the state sixty million dollars a year and would endanger federal aid to Texas because the national law had specified aid to the needy aged only.

Roy Sanderford of Belton, tax collector of Bell County for four years and a state senator for an equal length of time, was an anti-prohibitionist and a known friend and partisan of James E. Ferguson. He based his platform mainly on the need for a three percent state sales tax, arguing that such a levy would "hit the wealthy hardest." Late in the campaign he began to assert that he was the only candidate in the race who could defeat Allred in a runoff; "Hunter has lost twice, and Fischer is unknown and incompetent and is an oil millionaire," he told the voters.

Hunter, encouraged by his large vote in 1934, campaigned long and hard, criticizing the Allred administration at every opportunity. He blamed the governor for "cutting ribbons" and for financing old-age pensions through a liquor tax, either forgetting or ignoring the fact that Allred had made every possible plea for additional taxes in 1935. "The present set-up under Allred is neither adequate nor efficient," Hunter told one audience. "You can't aid the aged by drinking yourself into delirium tremens, yet only through booze can the aged be benefitted under the present system." At the close of his campaign Hunter predicted that he would lead the nearest candidate by a plurality of at least fifty thousand votes in the primary.

F. W. Fischer, like Hunter, entered the race early and conducted a long and aggressive campaign. Also like Hunter, he denounced and criticized Allred continually. His own revenue-raising scheme was an increased tax on oil, which he declared would reduce the gasoline tax, eliminate the ad valorem tax for state purposes, and "pay teachers' salaries commensurate with their training and service."

Pierce Brooks, a Dallas businessman, promised a more efficient administration of the state's affairs should he be elected chief executive. He proposed to curb the expansion of the government into new fields and said he would finance old age pensions through a gross receipts tax.

As the race drew to a close, each candidate began predicting victory, or at least a spot in the runoff. However, in 1936 there was no need for a second primary between the top two candidates; Allred secured a majority vote in the July election. Results showed that Allred was the preference of 553,219 Texans; Hunter, 239,460; Fischer, 145,877; Sanderford, 81,877; and Brooks, 33,391. The July primary set a new record high for the number of voters going to the polls, reaching above a million for the second time in history.

Between the July primary when Democratic nominees for office were selected and the inauguration of election winners in January, the old-age pension problem became more acute, making it necessary for Governor Allred to call a third special session of the legislature. When the program of assistance for the aged was first voted into being, the experts had predicted that probably about sixty-three thousand persons would apply for help. By September 1, 1936, however, the number had already reached eighty-one thousand, and the commission administering the program estimated that within a year there would probably be 150,000 on the state rolls. The third called session, which met in the fall of 1936, followed the advice of the governor by tightening the law somewhat in order to decrease the number who were eligible for assistance, and it complied with Allred's request for additional funds by setting aside approximately eight million dollars annually for pensions. To finance this program, the called session levied increased taxes on oil, gas, sulfur, carbon black, liquor, and other selected items.

Another item of importance that occurred between the July primary and the inauguration in January was the general election in November. There was no doubt as to the winners of the election; Democratic nominees always triumphed. But in November 1936 the voters were called to pass upon several more constitutional amendments. Among other things, they ratified salary increases for the governor and other high officials of the state; the pardoning power was transferred from the governor to the Board of Pardons and Paroles; larger counties were limited to seven representatives each, no matter how many residents they had; a teacher retirement system was authorized; and a workman's compensation insurance plan was approved.

In addition to these amendments, many of which necessitated the spending of more state funds, Allred found when the Forty-fifth Legislature convened in January 1937 that the public schools and colleges were expecting liberal support, the prison population was increasing rapidly because of a conservative pardoning policy and a tightening of law enforcement, and the number of patients in the state hospitals and charitable institutions was increasing by some five hundred a year. All these items were coupled with the Centennial expenditures, the interest and principal payments on the relief bonds of 1932, the increased aid to rural schools, a partial restoration of state salaries paid before the depression, and the rapid expansion of pensioners. Allred estimated that the state needed about $6,375,000 a year in additional revenues.

In his message to the new legislature, the governor referred the lawmakers to his 1935 speech to the Forty-fourth Legislature on finance and declared that his views were unchanged. He suggested that taxes be levied "on the 45 percent of our state property now escaping" and, in addition, suggested increased taxes on natural resources.

Despite the call of the governor for action on the financial front, the legislators in the 1937 regular session did nothing to solve the fiscal problems of the state. A proposed constitutional amendment permitting a sales tax to be collected and a bill to outlaw racetrack gambling failed to pass the Senate. Senator Hobart Nelson of Lubbock submitted a plan to provide for a one-house legislature in Texas, but after a spirited fight the proposal was defeated, greatly to the disappointment of many progressive citizens and editors. On the positive side, the Forty-fifth Legislature did establish a teacher retirement system, make some improvements in liquor regulation, pass a soil conservation bill, and enact a stronger drivers' license law.

Because the legislature was so generous in the appropriations bill, Allred felt it necessary to veto large sums in order to bring the budget within the range of the state's estimated income. And, as usual, he found it necessary to call a special session to provide the needed revenue to finance existing state obligations. Meeting in September 1937, the legislature became hopelessly deadlocked in its effort to raise money. The Senate passed a tax bill, but the House refused to concur. Instead it voted to liberalize the pension law. Finally the special session adjourned without having increased the state's income in any way. "A pitiful show of impotence," Alonzo Wasson of the Dallas *News* labelled the special session, which ended with the general revenue fund showing a deficit of thirteen million dollars.

Despite the financial difficulties which the state experienced under Governor Allred, his administration was fairly successful. Times were not as good as they had been during the twenties, but they were better than they had been under Sterling and Mrs. Ferguson during the early thirties. Governor Allred could retire from the governorship happy with the thought that his had been an honest and sincere effort and that the people of the state were relatively grateful for his work.

9

Showmanship in Politics

ACROSS THE LONE STAR STATE newspaper editors smiled politely; businessmen allowed themselves an amused chuckle; and professional politicians laughed outright when on May 1, 1938, a Fort Worth radio announcer and flour salesman announced his candidacy for the Democratic nomination for governor. They could be excused for their refusal to take the new candidate seriously, for he had no campaign manager, no headquarters, no knowledge of politics—in fact, he self-admittedly had never paid a poll tax or voted.

But within two and a half months the editors, businessmen, and politicians were united in attacking the newcomer as the leading contender in the race. To the surprise of these "experts," the man was drawing to his rallies the largest crowds in Texas political history, and

newspaper polls across the state showed that he undoubtedly would make the runoff.

Just who is this man? the astonished experts wanted to
know. Their second question was: How does he do it?

Gradually the facts emerged.

Wilbert Lee O'Daniel, a native of Ohio who had spent
much of his adult life in Kansas in the flour business, had
moved to Texas in 1925 to become sales manager and general manager of a Fort Worth milling firm. By 1938 he
was president of his own company, marketing his product
under the unlikely name of "Hillbilly Flour." His worth
was estimated at half a million dollars, and he had been
elected president of the Fort Worth Chamber of Commerce. Personally, however, he considered himself an
actor.

O'Daniel was a shrewd salesman who early recognized
the possibilities of radio. In 1927 he had organized a noon
weekday radio program employing three hillbilly musicians, whom he called the Light Crust Doughboys.
O'Daniel, himself, became master of ceremonies. On this
show he told housewives how to mend broken dishes and
broken hearts, sang hillbilly and religious music, recited
such poems as "The Boy Who Never Got Too Old To
Comb His Mother's Hair," told stories of national and
Texas heroes, gave advice on morals, safety, and thrift,
and sold flour. The show started with the call, "Please
pass the biscuits, Pappy," and soon he was affectionately
known to thousands of listeners as "Pappy" Lee O'Daniel.
Gradually the Light Crust Doughboys became better
known and were in demand in other towns for musical
programs. For such out-of-town shows, O'Daniel got an
old bus and fitted it with a loudspeaker; in this convey-
ance they travelled widely, further spreading the fame
of "Pappy" Lee O'Daniel. Through the years the musicians

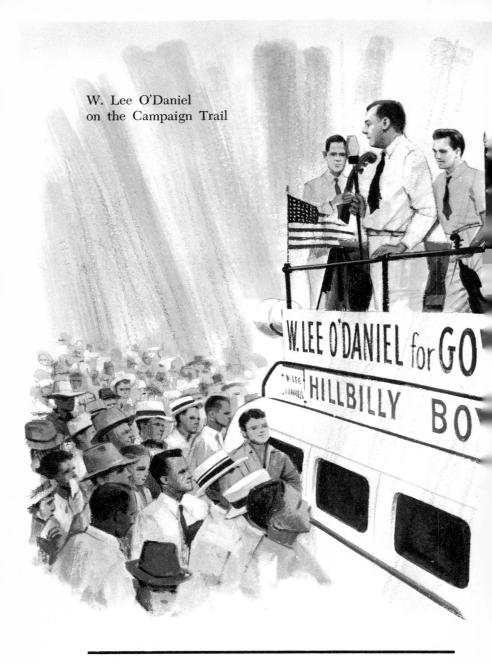

W. Lee O'Daniel
on the Campaign Trail

W. LEE O'DANIEL for GO'
HILLBILLY BO'

came and went and the programs varied in content, but the audience stayed with O'Daniel, leading one of his contemporaries in the radio business to declare, "He's just a born actor."

On his Palm Sunday broadcast in 1938 O'Daniel read a letter reportedly written by a blind admirer asking that he enter the Democratic primary and seek the nomination for governor. O'Daniel declared that he thought the idea was ridiculous, but he asked that his audience write in and help him make a final decision. A week later he said he had received 54,449 replies "begging" him to enter the contest, while three persons had written that he was "too good to waste himself on the job." On May 1 he told his radio listeners that he would enter the contest; his platform would be the Ten Commandments, his motto the Golden Rule.

A week later he told of an additional motto: "Less Johnson grass and politicians; more smokestacks and businessmen." On the same broadcast he explained how he planned to finance his campaign—the audiences at his rallies would be asked to contribute. "I say to you in all sincerity . . . , you had better take that old rocking chair down and mortgage it and spend the money in the manner you think best. . . . We have not one dollar in our campaign fund."

Travelling in the bus with the loudspeaker, he set out to talk with the voters of the state. His campaigning rules were simple: to entertain his audiences, to promise a thirty-dollar-a-month pension to every Texan over sixty-five years old, and to deride "professional politicians." His children went along on the campaign trail, his two sons playing in the band, his daughter passing the collection plates he had made in the form of barrels and labelled "Flour—Not Pork." Mrs. O'Daniel stayed home and ran his campaign from the dining room of the family residence in Fort Worth.

When asked how he would run Texas under his platform, the Ten Commandments, he would smile and declare, "Well, take the fourth commandment, Honor Thy Father and Thy Mother: Doesn't that mean old-age pensions just as plain as day?" Skeptics asked where the forty million dollars to finance this program would come from; O'Daniel would reply that he intended to attract new industries to the state, and taxes from them would cover the cost. When taunted about not paying a poll tax, he replied, "No politician in Texas is worth $1.75." On another occasion he declared "no sensible person" would vote for a "politician."

His clinching argument to the large audiences who came to hear him was equally simple—"Go ahead and try me for two years. You can't be any worse off than you have been." Actually, however, there is evidence to indicate that O'Daniel was not serious when he entered the primary. A reporter asked what he thought of his chances of election just before the primary was held; O'Daniel replied, "I don't know whether or not I'll get elected, but, boy! it sure is good for the flour business."

Robert Hicks of the Fort Worth *Star-Telegram* wrote from Sherman on June 22 to describe O'Daniel's tactics:

> The rally opens with hillbilly songs, then the candidate tells the crowd that the singing is over, and anyone who came for the show alone can leave. But no one does. He admits that when he first started talking about running he was simply looking for a new way to help sell his flour. But when the people became serious about it he did so too.
>
> O'Daniel is as mystified as his opponents in regard to his large crowds. . . .

Other candidates in the race, and there were thirteen in all, included William McCraw of Dallas, who was attorney general from 1934 to 1938 and was regarded early in the contest as the certain winner; Ernest O. Thompson of Amarillo, a railroad commissioner who had championed lower freight rates for farmers and stockmen and lower gas rates for consumers; and Tom Hunter, who was making his fourth bid for governor and who expected to win in 1938. With few variations the platforms of these three leading contenders were very similar: economy in government, no increase in taxes, and payment of the state's social security obligations. Thompson wanted lower utility rates throughout the state; McCraw favored a program of soil conservation; and Hunter urged the abolition of overlapping departments of the state government.

The campaign got under way very slowly during May and early June. Newspapers and leading citizens were predicting that the runoff would be between McCraw and Thompson, with someone occasionally substituting the name of Hunter for one or the other of them. During those first weeks practically no notice was taken of the O'Daniel candidacy. On May 8 the Fort Worth *Star-Telegram* casually and briefly noted that among the many candidates for governor was "W. Lee O'Daniel, the radio entertainer, who has formally announced." Thompson was drawing good-sized crowds of citizens, who listened respectfully to his discussions of the issues; McCraw was speaking to somewhat smaller groups against "the persistent movement for a sales tax"; Hunter, over a statewide radio hookup, was promising to save the taxpayers fifteen million dollars annually by eliminating useless commissions and bureaus in Austin.

Then toward the middle of June the O'Daniel tour began to take effect. At Waco he was greeted by a "huge crowd" which the Dallas *Times-Herald* declared was the largest to assemble in that town since Pat Neff had closed his campaign there against Joe Bailey eighteen years earlier. Moving westward, the O'Daniel soundtruck stopped in Abilene and Ballinger. In San Angelo friends of O'Daniel asserted that eight thousand people had gathered and that there had been "nothing like it in fifty years." At Colorado City on June 15 three thousand citizens waited three hours to hear him after bus trouble had delayed his arrival. At Childress a few days later another huge crowd greeted him, and by that time the press began to take notice, as did the other candidates. Some laughed at his "homely ideas about hillbilly campaigning," while others wished aloud that he had started a real upheaval against professional politicians.

And still the O'Daniel soundtruck moved through Texas. At Denton his audience was estimated as four times as large as any assembled there in recent years; at Gainesville the crowd was the largest gathered in that city since Joe Bailey had spoken there in his race for governor in 1920; and at Sherman an estimated ten thousand heard him speak.

Late in June the other candidates began to center their attacks on Pappy. McCraw was the most severe and persistent, calling the newcomer to politics his "flour-man friend" and said, "The big town hillbilly candidate . . . is no more a hillbilly than he is a student of government." In Georgetown he declared: "The banjo man from Fort Worth talks a great deal about home and religion and the Ten Commandments and the fine women of our state, but he doesn't say a word in his talks about gambling on horses, or selling liquor by the drink, or any other thing

our church people want to know about." At Buffalo, Mc-
Craw summed up his attitude about O'Daniel by observ-
ing, "A businesslike farmer does not employ a field hand
because he is a good crooner, nor does a sick man select
a doctor because he is a good tap dancer. . . . One candidate is offering thirty dollars a month pensions without
pretending to show how to raise the $40,000,000 a year or
more to pay them."

Candidate Thompson closed at Dallas before a large
crowd, predicting that he would win a majority of the
votes. O'Daniel, who had been freely making the same
prediction about himself, made his final speech at Fort
Worth, speaking on the grass slope west of the Municipal
Auditorium. A light rain fell during most of the program,
but the crowd remained to hear Texas Rose and Leon
Huff sing mountain music and "Pappy" give his speech.
In his part of the program, O'Daniel emphasized again
his plan for a businesslike administration, saying he would
seek the advice of a "council of business advisors."

The totals, when announced, showed that O'Daniel had
received 573,166 votes; Thompson, 231,630; McCraw,
152,278; Hunter, 117,634; and the other nine candidates
about 40,000 all together. For the third time in the biennial July primary a record number of votes had been cast,
and for the second time in a row there was no need for
a runoff to determine the nominee for governor. O'Daniel
had carried 231 counties and led all his opponents combined by some thirty thousand votes.

As shown in W. Lee O'Daniel and Texas Politics the
new governor's greatest majorities came from a hundred
mile radius of the Ft. Worth radio station, WBAP. Thus
had the new medium of communication made itself felt
and thus had O'Daniel utilized it to its fullest.

After it was certain that he had been nominated, Pappy

was offered $12,500 a week for ten weeks of personal appearances by an enterprising promoter. Friends urged him to accept the offer, but he declined, saying that he had to study for his new job.

The July primary had failed to settle the question in the race for six state offices, and a runoff had to be staged to determine the Democratic nominees. On July 26, O'Daniel announced that he would not take sides in any of the contests, but two weeks later in a radio broadcast he named the six men he wanted selected. During the final two weeks of the runoff, he urged his friends and supporters to vote for the candidates he preferred. And he was fifty percent successful; three of his choices were nominated, and three were defeated.

After the August primary, O'Daniel turned his attention to a review of taxation in Texas. It was agreed by fiscal experts that the state's obligation under the new social security program, including pensions for the aged, aid to the blind, help for indigent children, and a teachers' retirement system, would require some $48,000,000 to $60,000,000 a year in new taxes if the treasury were to erase the existing deficit and operate on a cash basis. Since O'Daniel had repeatedly denounced the sales tax plan, it was expected by most legislators that he would ask for an income tax. However, he did not consult with the lawmakers, and he refused to give any inkling of his plans before he was inaugurated.

Another incident which angered the legislators somewhat was O'Daniel's determination to appoint an unofficial "cabinet" of business advisors to aid him in running the government. He named some thirty Texans to his board late in November, and a week later in Fort Worth he held a banquet for this group. A group of legislators, who happened to be in Austin when the invitations to the banquet were sent, declared that O'Daniel's procedure "showed a total disregard for the legislature as well as ignorance of governmental processes." Clearly the new governor was not getting off to a good start with the men who would enact or reject his program.

The O'Daniel inauguration was attended by a crowd estimated at 100,000, one of the largest ever. After taking the oath of office, O'Daniel turned to his audience and said, "I pray that glamor and color will be eliminated from our legislative session and that seriousness and dignity will reign supreme." And to this crowd he gave his plan for new revenue, a "transactions tax" of 1.6 percent. He would abolish the ad valorem tax and reimburse the school fund for its losses thereunder with money from the cigarette tax. Again he called for pensions to those over sixty-five who did not have an income over thirty dollars a month. He concluded by estimating that his program would bring into the state treasury about forty-five million dollars annually. One witness declared that O'Daniel's inaugural address "refuted all prophesies" and "astonished all beholders."

Legislators greeted the governor's "tax on transactions" plan with a visible lack of enthusiasm, as did the businessmen of the state who loudly denounced it. Within a few short weeks it was apparent that the proposal had little chance of passage, and two substitute measures were introduced. G. C. Morris of Greenville, along with forty-three Representatives, brought before the House a natural resources tax bill, which they estimated would raise sixteen million dollars a year in new money, and Senator

R. A. Weinert of Seguin countered with a proposal in the upper chamber, calling for a two percent tax on all retail sales, which he felt would bring in thirty million dollars annually.

The Senate acted first. The Weinert sales tax plan, after amendments to include certain severance taxes on natural resources, was passed on April 10 under the title Senate Joint Resolution 12 and was sent to the House. O'Daniel in his broadcasts over a period of several weeks championed the Weinert measure and sought to have the people bring pressure on the House members to accept it, but fifty-six of the Representatives organized a bloc to kill the bill. This so-called "56 Club" was able to defeat Senate Joint Resolution 12 on ten separate roll call votes. Since the Senate likewise refused to accept the Morris proposal, no new revenue-raising measure passed the 1939 regular session.

Despite the governor's efforts, his threats, his entreaties, and his propaganda, his legislative program had failed in all its features. The nearest the legislature came to giving him what he wanted was a pensions liberalization bill which added eighty thousand names to the relief rolls. This addition naturally put a heavy strain on the treasury, which had a deficit of some twenty million dollars in the general revenue fund when O'Daniel entered office. He vetoed more than five million dollars from the appropriations bill passed by the legislature, but still the deficit continued to increase.

During the remaining months of 1939 various organizations sought to persuade the governor to call a special session of the legislature to finance pensions for every Texan over sixty-five, but his answer was a flat refusal. "If they could pass neither a statutory tax bill nor a constitutional amendment in 163 days at a cost of nearly a million dollars," he answered, "why should they be called back for a special session?" He was able to reach the end of the year without succumbing to the pressures.

Early in the spring of 1940, speculation increased about the possible candidates for governor. Naturally this speculation first centered around W. Lee O'Daniel, for by established precedent the incumbent seeks reelection. But O'Daniel would say nothing about his plans; in fact, he chose to leave the impression that he might not be a candidate for a second term. His evident and highly advertised failure to get his financial and old age pension proposals adopted by the legislature, coupled with his loss of favor with many of the aged for disappointing them and his alienation of other and smaller groups made it absolutely certain that he would face stiff opposition for reelection should he enter the race.

First to venture into the troubled political waters in 1940 was Harry Hines, a state highway commissioner who announced in Austin on February 20. Next came Railroad Commissioner Jerry Sadler, who had been elected in 1938 despite O'Daniel's "nod" for an opponent in the runoff. Then on April 14 came a call for the Ferguson adherents to rally around Mrs. Ferguson for a third term; her announcement came as no surprise, for her husband had been carefully preparing the voters for it since January. She based her candidacy on support of Franklin D. Roosevelt, who likewise was seeking an unprecedented third term. Another returning veteran of gubernatorial contests was Ernest O. Thompson, at first a candidate for Congress, but who in May declared himself willing to serve the state from the governor's mansion.

O'Daniel, of course, had been watching these developments closely and was preparing the voters for his own decision. About the middle of February the governor began broadcasting weekly a statement that his many friends were urging him to seek reelection. Next came his promise that he would soon answer the question "which has been asked by my thousands of friends." His formal announcement came in a broadcast on April 3; again his platform was the Ten Commandments, and again he asked for the passage of a transactions tax to yield a revenue of $45,000,000 annually.

Since the state was far in debt, most candidates' platforms centered around methods of raising revenues. Hines advocated increasing taxes on oil, gas, sulfur, and large corporations; Sadler's proposals were nearly identical, but he did not suggest taxing corporations. Mrs. Ferguson wanted a gross-receipts tax of one-half percent to raise fifty million dollars annually, a reduction in the state budget, aid to tenant farmers, and liberal support of education. Thompson advocated an increase of five cents a barrel in the tax on oil, arguing that such an increase would adequately finance old age pensions; this plan became known as the "Nickel-for-grandma-program."

As was to be expected, the four contestants seeking to unseat Pappy centered their attacks on the O'Daniel record. Jerry Sadler made an aggressive campaign, borrowing the governor's tactics by hiring a hillbilly band and several football stars to accompany him. He persistently criticized the O'Daniel administration, pointing out that during O'Daniel's eighteen months in office the state debt had increased by ten million dollars. Sadler said that although the governor had adopted the Ten Commandments as his platform and the Golden Rule as his motto, he was calling his opponents "vipers, snakes, liars, and hypocrites."

Thompson made a campaign of only three weeks, beginning his rallies on July 4. From every stump he attacked the O'Daniel record and repeatedly asked why O'Daniel had not joined the service in World War I. Thompson made known his opposition to a sales tax or transactions tax; he advocated soil conservation and repeal of the poll tax prerequisite for voting.

Texans with long memories must have breathlessly awaited a clash between Ferguson and O'Daniel. Both were colorful and adroit campaigners; both appealed to the rural element; and both knew how to please and entertain an audience. But the year was 1940, not 1914 or even 1924. Much of the Ferguson sparkle and zip was gone, and Mrs. Ferguson's campaign was more token than real.

O'Daniel varied his tactics from his 1938 sensation, especially during the first weeks. He centered his attack mainly on the various state agencies in Austin, declaring in his opening address in Waco on July 2 that these boards were "powerful oligarchies and juicy play-pretties for professional politicians." He suggested that his Waco address might be the only one he would make during the campaign, saying the governor was a very busy man. He berated his opponents who were state officials for "going about the state criticizing the governor instead of aiding him in his work." He condemned severely the 56 Club, which he labelled "a little bunch of pin-headed legislators," saying he would "clean house" in Austin if reelected.

The newspapers in 1940 were almost uniformly against the reelection of O'Daniel. Lynn Landrum of the Dallas *News* wrote, "The highest office in this state has been the laughingstock of the United States for a year and a half. If you have travelled out of Texas you know that is true; if you haven't you have a new experience in shame ahead of you. . . ." George Winningham, editor of the Harper

Herald, declared, ". . . we believe that O'Daniel is trying to stir up the old wet and dry issue to divert attention
away from the miserable failure he has made as a business
governor. . . ." A month later Winningham predicted that
the "political radio gabber is headed for the political
graveyard."

Late in the campaign the newspaper editors of the state
made a comprehensive effort through polls to determine
the outcome of the race. Raymond Brooks of the Austin
American-Statesman was given all the information
gathered for correlation; his prediction, released on July
25, was that O'Daniel would receive about forty-five percent of the vote and would be forced into a runoff with
Thompson or Hines. But such was not the case, for returns
for the July primary showed O'Daniel had received
645,646 votes; Thompson, 256,923; Hines, 119,121; Ferguson, 100,578; and Sadler, 61,396. Again O'Daniel had led
in almost every county, and again he had won the nomination without a runoff; his opponents combined received
102,002 fewer votes than he did.

Political turmoil did not end with the primary, for many
thoughtful Texans were concerned with avoiding a repeti-
tion of the deadlock between governor and legislature that
had occurred in the 1939 session; the state desperately
needed new sources of revenue to meet its social security
obligations. Everyone could agree on that point; the difficulty lay in finding a source acceptable to all. Dr. George
C. Hester, a professor of government at Southwestern
University and a former legislator, made a series of
speeches over the state in the summer of 1940 urging the
reorganization of the state government in the interest of
economy. He cited statistics to show that expenditures

during the past five years had risen by sixty-six percent, while population had risen by only five percent and the average family income not at all. These facts, declared Dr. Hester, showed that the real need was not new taxes but economy. Soon regional chambers of commerce and leading public speakers joined in the call for a reduction in state expenditures. The Joe Belden Poll, well known for its accuracy in sounding out Texas opinion, published in January 1941 its report on attitudes about taxation, showing that twenty-eight percent of the people questioned favored a sales tax, sixty-four percent wanted a resources tax, and eight percent desired neither.

Despite these manifestations of public opinion, O'Daniel submitted to the new legislature a tax program to raise sixty-one million dollars in new taxes annually; this included a 1.6 percent transactions tax, which would raise fifty million dollars, and an omnibus bill on natural resources and public utilities, to raise an additional eleven million dollars. Reporters, after an exhaustive investigation, estimated that not more than five senators and twenty-five representatives would support the governor's program.

The reporters were correct in their assessment. The governor's natural resources tax bill was introduced, but died in the Committee on Revenue and Taxation; the O'Daniel's transactions tax bill rested in committee for two and one-half months, and an effort to bring it out for special consideration was killed in the House on April 15 by a vote to 29 to 99. James E. Taylor of Kerens introduced a bill to impose a two percent sales tax, calculated to raise thirty-five million dollars annually, and another representative introduced an income tax bill, expected to bring in twenty-five million dollars a year, but both proposals likewise died in committee.

The major tax bill of the House was introduced by G. C. Morris and twenty others, mainly members of the "56 Club" of the preceding legislature; this plan called for an increase in the taxes on oil, gas, and sulfur, a tax of one percent on retail sales of automobiles, an increase from $1.50 to $2.00 a thousand on cigarettes, and a levy on gross receipts of insurance companies, telephone companies, and gas and light companies. The Morris Omnibus Tax Bill, as the measure became known, was reported out of the House Committee on Revenue and Taxation by a unanimous vote on March 3. Governor O'Daniel, who had been hoping to see his own proposal enacted, denounced the Morris Bill in his broadcast of March 9: "They received a bill sponsored by one of the leaders of the old gang of 56ers, and it is called an omnibus bill and is patterned after the old stinking S.J.R. 12." He called on new members of the House to "rise up and fight the Morris bill."

But the legislators chose to ignore the governor's call, for the next day, March 10, the House passed the Morris Bill by a vote of 136 to 8. A month and a half later the Senate likewise accepted the plan; the vote in the upper chamber was 31 to 0. This amounted to a legislative rebuke to the state's chief executive, and it helped precipitate a political crisis. Politics had suddenly become uppermost in the minds of Texas voters when a vacancy occurred in the United States Senate.

United States Senator Morris Sheppard, author of the Eighteenth Amendment and sixty-five-year-old dean of Congress, died on April 9, 1941. Sheppard had been a noteworthy member of the Senate, and Texans were sobered by a desire to see a suitable man replace him and serve the nation at a time of grave international problems.

According to the laws of the state and nation, the

governor could appoint a temporary successor to fill the vacancy, and a special election was to be called not less than sixty nor more than ninety days after the seat became vacant. Immediately there was widespread speculation as to the identity of the next senator; and in rumors, reports, and guesses, O'Daniel was always the key figure. The newspapers were full of suggestions that the safe procedure for the governor would be to retain the one office while campaigning for the other, resigning as chief executive after he had won the Washington office.

Representative Mark Halsey, Jr., of Lubbock introduced a resolution in the House on April 10 "respectfully requesting" O'Daniel to resign as governor and accept a temporary appointment to fill the Senate vacancy. The resolution was adopted by a large vote; O'Daniel's friends voted for the measure, feeling it would be a promotion, while foes supported the resolution in the hope that such a step would remove O'Daniel from Texas politics.

Other men recommended by various newspapers, speakers, and politicians included Congressmen Lyndon Johnson, Martin Dies, Wright Patman, Fritz Lanham, and former Vice-President John N. Garner. Such guesses and speculation, recommendations and denunciations, praise and abuse continued until Governor O'Daniel let it be known that the special election would be held on June 28 and that during his San Jacinto Day address from the monument he would name an interim senator to fill the vacancy.

On April 21 a large crowd attended the ceremonies at the battleground where the independence of Texas had been won. O'Daniel's speech was largely a eulogy to the achievements of General Sam Houston, leader of the Texan forces on that eventful day in 1836, and a recounting of the accomplishments of the hero's work in the

United States Senate. Near the close of his address he announced the appointment as temporary senator the only surviving son of Sam Houston, Andrew Jackson Houston.

This appointment raised a storm of indignation and protest from all parts of the state and from all factions except that one which assumed that Pappy Lee O'Daniel could do no wrong; the new senator lacked only a few weeks of being eighty-seven years old and was so feeble that it was doubtful that he would risk making the trip to Washington. Many indignant Democrats pointed out that Houston had been the Republican candidate in 1892 against James S. Hogg for governor and that he had been appointed a United States marshal by Republican President Theodore Roosevelt. However, it was almost unanimously assumed that the appointment of Houston indicated that O'Daniel expected to be a candidate in the special election, for the governor had selected as temporary senator a man who would not and could not oppose him.

Senator Houston did make the trip to Washington and thus became the oldest man ever to enter the Senate. He took the oath of office on June 2, 1941, almost a hundred years after his father had taken the same oath. The new senator enjoyed his honor only a few days; he appeared in the Senate chamber three times and attended one committee meeting. On June 20 he was taken to Johns Hopkins Hospital in Baltimore for a checkup and died there less than a week later following an operation for a stomach ailment.

Many prominent Texans thoughtfully considered the prospect of going to the Senate, but did not enter the contest. Former Governor Dan Moody was urged to run by several prominent men, but he had built a lucrative law practice in Austin and declined. Congressman Wright Patman of Texarkana almost filed as a candidate, but after

Lyndon Johnson entered the contest he decided to support the Central Texan instead. Lynn Landrum of the Dallas *News* repeatedly urged John Nance Garner to make the race, but the former Vice-President took no notice and said nothing. James Ferguson gave strong indication that he might become a candidate; already sixteen names had been filed, and according to Texas law at that time only a plurality was needed to win in the special election. "Our crowd can put it over," Ferguson declared at one point, but on May 10 he announced that he would not be a candidate. He said he and his wife would vote for O'Daniel should the governor enter the contest; otherwise he declared the Ferguson choice would be the man who would do the least harm in Washington.

Still, there was no shortage of candidates, a total of twenty-nine filing for the post. Twenty-five of these men were minor candidates and polled an aggregate vote of less than fifty thousand. The four major candidates included Gerald C. Mann, attorney general of the state and a native of Sulphur Springs; Martin Dies of Orange, who had served for ten years in Congress and was well known for his work on the House Un-American Activities Committee; Lyndon Johnson, a congressman from Central Texas known as a supporter of the Roosevelt administration; and W. Lee O'Daniel, colorful governor of Texas.

On April 12, the day Senator Sheppard was buried, an editorial appeared in the Austin *Tribune* advising the people to write or wire Governor O'Daniel if they wished him to run for the Senate. It spoke of the "widespread and spontaneous demand" for O'Daniel to accept the office, complimented him on his record as governor, and asserted that his election would bring "invaluable prestige" to the state. Two days later O'Daniel addressed the

House; he thanked the members for their vote of confidence as contained in the Halsey resolution which asked him to be a candidate for the Senate, and he suggested a five-point program which—if enacted—would justify his retirement as governor to become a senator. The program included new taxes of forty million dollars annually to finance old age pensions, the submission of a constitutional amendment forbidding deficit spending, abolition of the poll tax as a prerequisite for voting, the passage of a bill providing for a state auditor-budget director, and the abolition of capital punishment for crime.

During the following three weeks the legislature did little to satisfy the governor's requests. Nevertheless, O'Daniel announced in a broadcast on May 19 that he would seek the Senate seat. He declared that "we got the job done" as governor, assuring his listeners that he would take with him to Washington the Ten Commandments, the Golden Rule, and "a common touch with the common man." No mention was made of resigning as governor before the election. When reporters reminded him of his criticisms of Hines, Sadler, and Thompson in 1940 for running for one office while holding another and asked if he would resign as governor, he replied, "I should say not."

Not until June did the campaign really get under way. O'Daniel was delayed by the "stubbornness of the legislature" which refused to adjourn and go home, Johnson by a throat infection, Mann by planning and organizing a very heavy campaign, and Dies by his decision to make few speeches.

O'Daniel opened his bid early in June in Waco with the usual hillbilly band, sound truck, soloists, members of his family, and small flour barrels for contributions. His crowd of 5,500 was disappointingly small, and when rain began falling about 5,000 of that number left. The governor told his audience that he would be of real help to "that boy" in Washington, referring to President Roosevelt. And he said he would try to prevent a rise in the public debt by introducing a new tax bill for every appropriation bill passed.

Later in his campaigning, O'Daniel added such refinements to his promises as a declaration that he would "purge" from the Senate anyone who failed to support an "anti-strike bill" which he would introduce, and he declared he would keep Texas politicians on the national scene "on probation."

Johnson campaigned largely on support of the President's foreign policy. In his first speech, given at San Marcos on May 3 before seven thousand people, he declared the country was in more danger than it had been at any time since the Declaration of Independence was signed. He urged his listeners to stand behind the President, to support a rapid program of preparedness, and to instruct their representatives to vote for aid to England as a means of preserving American democracy. Johnson made heavy use of the airplane during the contest, flying about the state to his many rallies. He called attention to the polls which showed he was making steady gains; he stressed the need for support of the Roosevelt administration; and he urged that his experiences had qualified him for the office of senator. More and more he came to rely on Roosevelt's support, and telegrams were read at his rallies to the effect that he was the President's choice for the office. He freely admitted that he would be a "yes-man" to Roosevelt on questions of national unity.

Gerald Mann covered the state diligently, making over

three hundred speeches in all. He declared that the race was really between himself and the governor and reminded his audiences that in the 1938 Democratic primary he had received 130,000 more votes in his race for attorney general than O'Daniel had for governor. And Mann criticized the federal officials who were in Texas campaigning for Johnson.

Dies castigated all his opponents, but most of all he took O'Daniel to task for his "medicine show campaign tactics." He said that Texas should not send to Washington a man who had to "have a hillbilly band play for him while he has to stop and think." He declared that the President "does not need a green man, a yes man, or a show man" to help him in the Senate, referring to his own experience, independence, and dignity.

O'Daniel scheduled the usual "victory party" for Saturday election night on the mansion lawn, but the party lagged somewhat about midnight when returns showed that Johnson was leading by some three thousand votes. Two days later Johnson's lead had increased to five thousand with ninety-six percent of the votes counted. Barring a miracle, it appeared that the young congressman was the certain winner. The Sunday newspapers gave long and detailed biographical sketches of the "new senator," and congratulations poured in from over the state and nation. But during the fourth day of counting, the remote and small counties began sending in O'Daniel majorities, and the governor pushed ahead of his nearest opponent, building a slim lead that was maintained until the count was completed. The final tally was O'Daniel, 175,590; Johnson, 174,279; Mann, 140,807; and Dies, 80,551. O'Daniel was on his way to Washington.

The senator-elect planned to take the oath of office five weeks after the special election, thus leaving plenty of time to wind up his affairs in Texas. During this interim many Texas voters had misgivings and second thoughts about the type of reception Pappy would receive in Congress, for during the campaign he had censured the nation's lawmakers publicly and repeatedly. He had said that the President was surrounded by professional politicians who were incapable of running a peanut stand; he had declared that he would put the federal government on a cash basis, an unheard of idea in New Deal circles; he had told Texas audiences that he would introduce a bill to outlaw strikes and would broadcast the names of senators and representatives who refused to vote for his measure; and he had said it was his intention to "twist their tails down in Washington like I did the old cows on the ranch in Kansas." These promises and threats had been thoroughly advertised over the nation by the metropolitan newspapers and magazines, and fears that O'Daniel's reception would not be cordial were more than justified.

But if congressmen were alienated by O'Daniel's campaign statements, they were shocked by his disdain for senatorial customs and by his colorful tactics in the conservative upper house. The former Texas governor made his maiden speech on the second day of his membership, breaking the record of Huey Long of Louisiana who had scandalized the Senate by speaking to that body on the third day of his service. In the course of a twenty-five minute talk against extending the Selective Service Act, O'Daniel injected such irrelevancies as, "I do like hillbilly music. I also like popular music, church songs, and grand opera; but unfortunately I do not play or sing any kind of music. . . ."

Then O'Daniel began introducing his legislation. An anti-strike bill was sent to the Committee on the Judiciary,

as was his proposed constitutional amendment guarantee-
ing freedom to work (an anti-labor union measure). The
Texan declared in defending these measures that Congress was "almost completely ignoring the most serious
problem confronting the nation. . . . The ugly, dangerous
factor in our body politic today to which I refer is the
powerful dominating labor-union leader racketeers." In
another bill he introduced to promote and facilitate inter-
state commerce, O'Daniel asked for a federal ban on the
use of pipelines for transporting natural gas. He asked
for legislation to forbid the sale of liquor to soldiers and
to provide for the suppression of vice in the vicinity of
military camps and naval establishments. And he called
for an investigation into the production and distribution
of commercial fertilizers. However, not one O'Daniel
measure became law; in fact, when his proposals were
considered in regular calendar order, the majorities against
him were so overwhelming as to be embarrassing.

Nevertheless, early in 1942 O'Daniel announced that
he would be a candidate for reelection to the Senate that
year. He told Texans that he had backed every appropriation asked for by the President, and he promised to support every bill that would aid in winning World War II,
which had begun in December 1941.

Since the junior Texas senator had so narrowly escaped
defeat at the hands of Lyndon Johnson in the special election for the seat, since his many failures in the Senate had
been thoroughly publicized in Texas, and since it was
widely believed that O'Daniel was opposing the President's war measures, political experts both in Washington
and in Texas thought that there would be spirited opposition to him in the Democratic primary. And such was

the case, although it was more than a month after O'Daniel's announcement that former Governors Allred and Moody revealed their plans. Allred declared that he believed he would be able to serve his country in the Senate better than O'Daniel could and denounced O'Daniel's opposition to the war. Moody likewise stated that he would run on the basis of all-out support of the war effort.

From the press came happy sounds when the two former governors announced. Lynn Landrum of the Dallas *News* wrote, "This summer there will be a debate by men of distinction and ability. . . . It is here and now predicted that the Senator will have to go several steps beyond yodeling his way to renomination." And in the *New Republic*, a nationwide liberal magazine, was the comment, "Pappy is up against a very different and much more threatening situation than he had to deal with last year. O'Daniel will be asked to explain how he helped to win the last war by riding up and down the streets of a small Kansas town in a Ford he had painted red, white, and blue, advertising his flour. . . ."

Even O'Daniel declared his happiness at the announcements of Allred and Moody. He said that he had worried a great deal for fear that he would not have an opponent and thus would not get to return to Texas and have the pleasure of making a campaign. He asserted that he had been so worried at such a prospect that he had paced up and down the Senate corridors just like an expectant father; then "finally the news was announced and it was twins." Thereafter, throughout the campaign, he spoke of his opponents as the "Gold Dust Twins." O'Daniel announced that he would finance his campaign by passing the barrels again and that he would found a newspaper for the duration of the race; subscriptions to the *W. Lee O'Daniel News* would be one dollar each.

Despite the fact that the public mind was focused on international affairs and the war, the 1942 senatorial race was a spirited and exciting one. Both Moody and Allred hammered away at the theme, O'Daniel "ought not to go back" to Washington, and both asserted that support of the war—or lack of it—was the major issue of the campaign. Allred, considered the leading contender, declared in his opening address on May 15 over a statewide radio network that Texas was entitled to better representation in the Senate than O'Daniel was providing. "Texas must be mortified no longer," Allred stated, "our interests held back no longer by a Senator who cannot command the respect or cooperation of his associates in the Senate." Allred said his four main objectives, if elected, would be working to win the war, provide for the men in the service, plan the readjustments of our economic life, and write a peace that would insure the next generation against the tragedy of war.

Senator O'Daniel did not announce a definite platform at any time. Answering charges that he was an isolationist, that he had failed to support the war effort, O'Daniel declared, ". . . we can leave the handling of the war in the hands of our commander-in-chief. It does not enter into this race. . . . The matter of retaining our American form of democracy will be more important after the war is won." Speaking of the war itself, Pappy commented, "I am sure we have gone over the hump. It will be over sooner than you have been thinking."

Warming to his task, O'Daniel began his usual diatribes against professional politicians. "You folks just can't realize what it means to live in Texas until you have lived in a foreign country for a while, as I've been doing. . . .

Washington is the only lunatic asylum in the world run by its own inmates." During the latter part of July O'Daniel in almost every speech made a thinly veiled charge that Allred had been bribed by the "Communistic labor leader racketeers" to make the race for the Senate. By implication he asserted that Allred had been offered $200,000 by labor bosses to enter the contest and an additional $200,000 if he won. "Of course," he added, "I'm not going to say positively that the Communistic labor leader racketeers made such a deal. They didn't call me in on their meeting. But I'll let you form your own conclusions."

The leading newspapers of the state, with very few exceptions, editorially opposed the reelection of O'Daniel. The San Antonio *Express* favored Moody; all the Houston papers urged the election of Allred, and the Dallas *News*, Fort Worth *Star-Telegram,* and Lubbock *Avalanche-Journal* made no specific choice between Allred and Moody, contenting themselves with calling for the defeat of O'Daniel. The Dallas *News* went so far as to state that O'Daniel's campaign arguments were "an insult to the intelligence of Texans" and asked that the voters of the state "put an end to O'Danielism."

But Texans had minds of their own, and election totals were not what the editors had asked. O'Daniel received 475,541 votes; Allred, 317,501; and Moody, 178,471. O'Daniel had led in 220 counties, Allred in 31, and Moody in 3.

Once over their astonishment, editors began to analyze the returns. They decided that O'Daniel had led because practically all the older citizens of the state had stayed home during the war and had voted for their hero in large numbers, while the young men and women had left home to work in defense plants or serve in the armed forces and thus were unavailable to vote for their favorites, Allred and Moody. Further, the editors declared that Texans were no longer as much in sympathy with the Roosevelt domestic policies as they once had been and had reacted favorably to the O'Daniel pronouncements against labor racketeers and creeping federal control of business. Many Texans had believed that Allred was the White House favorite, even that Moody was more acceptable than O'Daniel to the President, and therefore they had supported O'Daniel.

The runoff differed from the July primary only in length and intensity. Senator O'Daniel campaigned just two weeks in the August contest, Allred three, and there was much vilification of personalities. Both candidates naturally made bids to secure the support of Dan Moody, who had been eliminated, but it was Allred who was successful. On August 18 the unsuccessful aspirant declared he would vote for Allred.

Since references to the "Gold Dust Twins" were no longer applicable, Pappy spoke of Allred as "My little yes-man opponent," and he insisted that in Washington he had supported all genuine war measures. Despite the O'Daniel campaign of only two weeks, the senator spoke extensively, making about six or seven appearances a day. He called his whirlwind effort an "appreciation tour" to thank the voters for their support. After O'Daniel had spoken fifty-two times in one week, the Dallas *News* quoted one citizen as saying the O'Daniel effort was "the most frantic appreciation tour on record."

Allred revised his platform somewhat during August to include support of higher prices for farm products and opposition to gasoline rationing in Texas, socialized medicine, federal control of oil, and regimentation of industry. But despite Moody's support and the new planks in his platform, Allred was defeated. The runoff totals were O'Daniel, 451,359; Allred, 433,203. O'Daniel had once again worked his magic.

However, when the senator returned to Washington, he found his colorful tactics were not appreciated. Winning the war had become the prime concern, not only of the officials of the federal government, but of the entire nation. For the first time in many years, politics had to take a back seat.

10

War and Prosperity

SUNDAY, DECEMBER 7, 1941, for most Texans began as a peaceful pre-Christmas day of worship. Suddenly that afternoon national radio networks and local stations interrupted their programs to bring the unexpected news of a surprise Japanese attack on American military installations at Pearl Harbor in Hawaii. Nineteen ships had been sunk and many lives lost.

Soon newspapers across the state had special editions on the streets, and citizens rushed to buy them to get additional details of the sneak bombing. Everywhere Texans grouped together to discuss the meaning of the event and to ponder about what the future held. Anxiously they awaited as developments unfolded. Monday morning, December 8, President Roosevelt went before Congress and called for a formal declaration of war, and the lawmakers readily responded. Three days later Germany and Italy, honoring their commitments to Japan, announced that the United States was thereafter to be included among the countries they were fighting.

The country was at war for the second time in the twentieth century!

Actually World War II had begun in Asia as early as 1931 and in Europe in 1939, and the federal government under Roosevelt had been taking steps to prepare Americans for possible entry into the contest. A peace-time draft law, the first in United States history, had been passed in September 1940, and lend-lease aid had been extended to England in its struggle with Germany. Public opinion was being shaped through the Committee To Defend America by Aiding the Allies, created in 1940 and headed by William Allen White. Still it came as a shock to most Americans when hostilities actually began.

On the morning of December 8, recruiting offices in the Lone Star State were crowded as Texans, as always, rallied to fight for the nation. No longer was there any talk of isolationism or pacifism; no longer was there any hesitation. All that was left were loyalty and a willingness to fight. Young men and women joined the armed forces, and the older ones rolled up their sleeves and prepared to work for victory on the farms or in the factories.

The national selective service laws were extended to require the registration of all men between the ages of eighteen and forty-five, but there was little immediate need for a draft act in the Lone Star State. In December 1942 Secretary of the Navy Frank Knox declared that Texas had contributed a larger percentage of its men to the armed forces than any other state. Out of a total population of about six and a quarter million, about 750,000 Texans served in the Army, Navy, Marine Corps, Coast Guard, and Merchant Marines, and twelve thousand women saw service in the auxiliary forces. The Thirty-sixth Division and Fifty-sixth Cavalry were all-Texan units and became world-famous for their fighting ability, while a high proportion of the members of the Nineteenth Division, First Cavalry Division, One Hundred Twelfth Cavalry Division, Second Infantry Division, and One Hundred Third Infantry Regiment were Texans. In these units as groups and in other commands as individuals, Texans saw service on all fronts and in all theaters of the war. Of the three quarters of a million who went off to war, 23,022 were killed in action or died of wounds, while thousands more were injured, crippled, or disabled.

Many Texans rose to national prominence during the conflict. The state contributed at least twelve admirals and 155 generals, including Chester W. Nimitz, commander in chief of the Pacific Fleet, and Dwight D. Eisenhower, Supreme Allied Commander in Europe. Directing the Women's Army Corps (WACS) was Colonel Oveta Culp Hobby, wife of the former governor. Thirty Texans won the Congressional Medal of Honor and six the Navy Medal of Honor, among whom were Lieutenant Audie Murphy, the "most decorated" soldier of World War II, and Commander Samuel D. Dealey, the "most decorated man in the Navy." Texans could well be proud of their fighting men.

As in World War I, the state was once again a center of training activities, a total of fifteen posts being located in the state for that purpose. The Third Army, which controlled basic training camps from Arizona to Florida, was headquartered at San Antonio, as was the Fourth Army, which readied men for overseas combat service through

advanced training bases in nine states. And later, as the war progressed, twenty-one camps for prisoners of war were constructed in the Lone Star State.

Throughout the war Texans had only to listen to know that their state was the center of the military aviation effort, for airplanes were almost constantly buzzing overhead. Randolph Field at San Antonio, often called the "West Point of the Air," had been completed in 1930 at a cost of eleven million dollars and proved its worth during the war years. Randolph, along with Kelly and Brooks fields, made San Antonio a hub of flying activity; other bases were hastily constructed or reactivated at Lubbock, Midland, Wichita Falls, San Angelo, San Marcos, Houston, and elsewhere to take advantage of the good flying weather and the relatively level terrain. The national headquarters of the Air Force Training Command was in Fort Worth at Carswell Field; in January 1944 it had under its direction more than one million men and women. In addition, there were various naval air training fields, including the vast complex at Corpus Christi, completed in 1941 at a cost of forty-four million dollars, and the primary flight training base at Grand Prairie. Between January 1, 1942, and May 1, 1944, more than 200,000 airmen were trained in Texas, including 45,000 pilots, 12,000 bombardiers, 12,000 navigators, and many aerial gunners, photographers, and mechanics.

At home the civilians became familiar with rationing stamps for their purchases of gasoline, meat, sugar, coffee, shoes, automobile parts, and other scarce items. They took part in scrap iron drives, during which junk heaps and trash dumps were scoured to furnish the desperately needed material. They grew "Victory Gardens" to conserve food. And they participated in numerous war bond drives; even school children bought war stamps, pasting them in books which when filled were exchanged for bonds.

Fortunately, there was little hatred or persecution of the so-called "hyphenated Americans" during the conflict. Few doubted but that the German element in Texas consisted of true citizens, and no Ku Klux Klan arose to whip recalcitrant civilians. Loyalty was taken for granted.

And the war accomplished what no government program of spending had been able to do during the thirties: it ended the Great Depression. Full employment returned and wages rose as private industry turned out the material of war and the farmers planted every possible acre. With so many air bases in the state, it was natural for aircraft factories to be built nearby; these included the Southern Aircraft plant at Garland, the North American Aviation factory at Grand Prairie, and the enormous Consolidated Aircraft Corporation complex near Fort Worth—reputed to be one of the largest factories of any kind in the world. The oil industry expanded to fuel the war machine, to run the factories and propel the tanks, airplanes, and ships; and the petrochemical industry came of age between 1941 and 1945. Synthetic rubber plants were constructed, and munitions plants mushroomed. Along the coast shipyards were enlarged and new ones started. The world's largest tin smelter was built at Texas City. And steel mills were erected at Daingerfield and Houston. Since so many of the men were in the armed forces, Texas women for the first time in the state's history went into the factories to become riveters, punch press operators, and assembly line workers.

Because so much of the world was at war during the first half of the forties, the United States was called upon to feed millions of non-Americans. Not only the civilians at home and servicemen at all the fronts, but foreign civilians and servicemen were dependent on American farmers for their daily meals. Mechanization and increased acreage utilization were the answer. In Texas the war brought several changes in the agricultural pattern, some of them blessings, some not so good.

No longer were cotton and cattle the kings they had been. Cotton acreage dropped from a peak of 17,749,000 in 1926 to 5,800,000 in 1945 and from sixty to thirty percent of the total value of all crops harvested in the state. Diversification became more than just a word during the war years, with approximately 135 crops being grown. Especially important were cotton, feed grains, rice, wheat, vegetables, and citrus fruits. Texas led in the production of cotton, grain sorghums, cattle, sheep, goats, horses, turkeys, tomatoes, onions, spinach, pecans, and roses. The

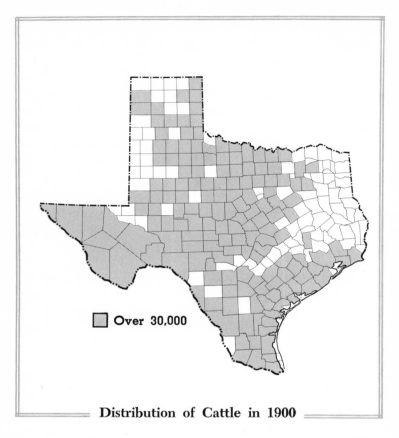

Distribution of Cattle in 1900

1945 agricultural census showed that the state ranked
fourth in farm income, trailing California, Iowa, and
Illinois; agricultural workers that year received $1,189,-
901,100 for their crops and livestock.

Other agricultural changes wrought by the war included
an increase in the average price per acre of Texas land
(from $18.81 to $25.29), a decrease in the total number
of farms (from 418,002 to 384,977), and a steady growth
in the use of machinery. (Total valuation of farm imple-

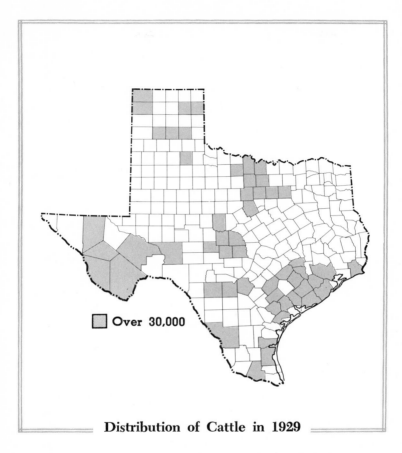

Over 30,000

Distribution of Cattle in 1929

ments and machinery in 1945 was $277,000,000, a gain of almost $100,000,000 since 1940.) There was an increased usage of irrigation to free farmers from the fear of drouth. And farm living conditions showed considerable improvement during the 1940's. Rural electrification brought the marvels of the twentieth century to remote areas of the state, and the farm-to-market road system made it possible for farmers and their families to travel quickly in all types of weather. Telephone lines and gas pipelines brought still more improvements in the rural way of life, so that by the late forties farmers enjoyed a standard of living about equal to that of city dwellers.

One startling change in the agricultural matters in Texas that largely escaped attention at the time was a gradual shift in ranching from West to East Texas. Until 1930 the normal procedure was for the rancher to retreat westward before the farmer, and the cattle population of the state steadily declined. With the start of the Great Depression and the oil boom east of the Brazos River, however, there was a revival of beef raising, especially in East Texas. In fact, by 1945 there were more cattle to be found in East Texas than in West Texas. For years county agents and agricultural experts had been preaching a "cow, sow, and hen" doctrine to the one-crop farmers in East Texas, and finally such work paid off. When the East Texans seriously turned to raising beef and dairy cattle, they encouraged native grasses, along with new and improved range grasses, to grow in their vacated cotton fields. Thus they developed pastures second to none.

With the income from crops, livestock, petroleum, minerals, and industry spiraling constantly upward, Texans prospered during the war. After the conflict came to an end, there was no depression, for the economy continued to boom. The hard times had definitely come to an end.

There was relatively little bitterness in Texas politics during the early forties, for prosperity made the voters content; besides, their attention was focused on the fighting fronts and international events. Coke Stevenson, the lieutenant governor, became the state's chief executive in August 1941 when W. Lee O'Daniel resigned to take a seat in the United States Senate, and Texans apparently were happy with him. In fact, Stevenson hardly found it necessary to campaign for reelection in the summers of 1942 and 1944. The wartime governor, a native of Kimble County, had behind him a successful career as a banker, rancher, county attorney, county judge, and legislator before he won the office of lieutenant governor. In contrast with the colorful O'Daniel, Stevenson was quiet and dignified, seldom became irritated or ruffled, and took his political ups and downs philosophically, for which he became known as "Calculating Coke." During his five years and five months in office, his popularity steadily increased.

The wartime unity in Texas politics came to an end in 1946, however, and two campaigns stirred the voters deeply in the immediate postwar world: the gubernatorial contest of 1946 and the senatorial race in 1948.

The outstanding issue in the election of 1946 was the firing in November 1944 of Homer Price Rainey from his position as president of the University of Texas. Dr. Rainey had been removed by the University Board of Regents because of a clash over administrative policy. Rainey contended that the board had no right to interfere in the University's internal affairs, a number of which had become controversial, while the board took the position that it was the legally constituted policy-setting body for the school.

An important fundamental principle was involved: Could the taxpayers of the state, whose money supported the institution, exercise control over it through their indirect representatives—the Board of Regents—or must the professional educators be given a free hand in the name of "academic freedom"? In the bitterness which followed, unfortunately, the basic issue was virtually lost. Professor Henry Nash Smith, a Rainey spokesman, discussed a dozen points of controversy in a pamphlet entitled *The Controversy at the University of Texas, 1939-1945*. He likened the fight for academic freedom to "the debates in the American colonies during the decade preceding the outbreak of the Revolution."

J. Evetts Haley, one of Texas' outstanding historians, became an outspoken protagonist for the board and defended its position in a similar pamphlet, *The University of Texas and the Issue*. To the candid cowboy-scholar, Rainey's public statements smacked of "emotional fervor" and "perversion of the truth." "It is not only the right," said Haley, "but the bounden duty of the board to govern the University. If the president needed firing, then the regents would have been derelict in duty had they not fired him." The principal question, as the participants saw it, was whether the president should have been dismissed. Rainey, with the fiery support of the liberal majority of the faculty, decided to take the issue to the people of the state. During the following eighteen months he spoke extensively, both in Texas and outside the state, explaining his side of the dispute. Early in the spring of 1946 he announced he would be a candidate for governor as a means of vindicating himself.

Railroad Commissioner Beauford Jester, his principal opponent in the gubernatorial campaign, was supported by the conservatives and rural elements. Other major candidates for the office in the primary included Attorney General Grover Sellers, Lieutenant Governor John Lee Smith, and Colonel Jerry Sadler, just discharged from the army. In addition, there were nine other "minor" aspirants for the position.

The Rainey campaign platform was an elaborate program for the improvement of education, health, old-age pensions, farm-to-market roads, and general social conditions in the state. The candidate called for increased taxes and spending, the money to come mainly from increased levies on natural resources. He advocated the industrialization of Texas, elimination of control of the state by the Texas Regulars (a splinter group of politicians who had fought Roosevelt and Truman reforms and civil rights legislation for Negroes), and a more careful check on the release of prisoners from the state penitentiary. Since Dr. Rainey was a controversial figure who had been much in the public eye for almost two years and since early polls showed him to be a leading contender for the office of governor, the other candidates centered their attacks on him. Rainey answered that the campaign of vilification against him was caused by his support of the Roosevelt administration.

Sellers, besides attacking Dr. Rainey, advocated extending to veterans long-term loans at low rates of interest to enable them to purchase farms and homes, and he castigated Jester for not resigning from the Railroad Commission while a candidate for governor. Sadler proposed a heavy tax on oil, gas, and sulfur, the money to be used to finance old-age pensions of forty dollars a month, better salaries for teachers, and a greatly expanded state health program. Smith contented himself with attacks on the former president of the University; he charged that Rainey leaned toward atheism, communism, and socialism.

Beauford Jester was perhaps shrewder than his fellow candidates, at least in gauging the mood of the electorate in the postwar years. His was not seeking of vindication nor a platform based on vilification. Instead he asserted that if he were elected, there would be no need for new or additional taxes to run the state. He promised to fight

Communist labor leaders, federal interference in state affairs, and the Political Action Committee (PAC) of the Congress of Industrial Organizations, a national labor union noted for its liberal leanings. Jester busied himself setting up local campaign committees all over the state, and he repeatedly complimented the Texas voters as the best informed in the country.

The results of the July primary showed that Jester's efforts had not been in vain. He polled 444,000 votes; Rainey, 291,000; Sellers, 162,000; Sadler, 103,000; and Smith, 102,820. The other nine candidates combined received about 60,000 votes. Jester had secured thirty-eight percent of the July total, Rainey twenty-five percent.

With the primary behind them, Jester and Rainey prepared to fight for the 428,000 votes which had been cast for the twelve defeated aspirants. It was widely known that a large percentage of the Sellers and Smith supporters favored a Jester victory; only Sadler asked the public to vote for Rainey, charging Rainey's opponents with "dirty politics." Governor Stevenson and former Governors Hobby, Mrs. Ferguson, Moody, and Sterling announced by the middle of August that they favored the election of Jester. Allred was the only former chief executive to back Rainey, while Neff and O'Daniel took no stand for either candidate. And the newspapers, in most cases, assessed the political picture correctly and forecast a Jester victory.

But Dr. Rainey was not one to quit without a fight. He vainly challenged Jester to a series of joint debates, he continued his road campaign throughout August, and he made every effort to overcome the Jester lead. He demanded that Jester should resign as railroad commissioner, and from every speaking platform he repeated that Texas was in the hands of the corporations and great monopolies and should be rescued. And he explained his discharge from the presidency of the University as due to politics; he was a Roosevelt supporter, he said, while the governor and practically all of the members of the Board of Regents were Texas Regulars.

Jester made a more conservative campaign, asserting that Rainey was seeking the office of governor only as a means of gaining revenge and that the ex-president of the University was trying to impose on the people a "new, radical, and expensive form of government." By his example, of a quiet and dignified approach, Jester helped the voters decide that Rainey was an impractical radical, as had been charged so often in the July primary.

The final Belden poll indicated that sixty-three percent of the voters preferred Jester, and the accuracy of the forecast was borne out a few days later. In the runoff election, Jester received 701,018 votes (sixty-six percent); Rainey 355,654 (thirty-four percent). The former University president led in only seven counties out of 254.

The general election in November 1946 followed the usual Texas pattern. The Democrats saw no need to make a campaign, and the Republicans felt it would be useless for them to do so. Nor did the voters show much enthusiasm, fewer than 400,000 of them going to the polls. Jester led his Republican opponent, Eugene Nolte, Jr., by a majority of ten to one.

The senatorial campaign of 1948 was an entirely different race, however. There were several distinguished candidates; it was a presidential election year; and the Republicans had some hope of carrying Texas in the general election. Ex-Governor Coke Stevenson was the first to announce that he would seek election to the O'Daniel seat. Declaring that his supporters could expect no political promises from him, Stevenson said he would stand on his past record, that he was in favor of economy, states' rights, individual freedom, social security, and aid to non-Communist nations, and that he would work in the federal government for the same sound fiscal policies he had followed in Texas. He asserted that when he came to office, the state had a thirty million dollar deficit; at the end of his tenure, the state had a thirty-five million dollar surplus.

Ten days later, George Peddy, a Houston lawyer, stated that he likewise would seek the O'Daniel Senate seat. Peddy had ventured into Texas politics only once previously; in 1922 he had been a write-in candidate of the anti-Klan faction against Earle B. Mayfield in the general election. Peddy said that if elected he would work for a solution of the difficulties between labor and management (there were many strikes during the early postwar years), a reduction of government spending through greater efficiency and the removal of "deadwood," a promotion of world peace through stronger American military power, a closer attention to the needs of veterans, and a federal recognition of Texas' claims to the oil-rich tidelands.

The third "major" candidate in the race was the loser in the 1941 special election for the same seat, Lyndon Johnson. The Central Texan had served as congressman from the Austin district since 1937 and was known as a hard worker and an ardent "New Dealer." He favored foreign aid, wanted a strong air force, more aid to the states to build hospitals, and higher pay for federal employees. Shortly after Pearl Harbor was bombed, Johnson had taken a leave of absence from Congress and had served in the navy for more than a year before President Roosevelt called him back to Washington.

A total of eight other Texans, the so-called "minor candidates," also sought the coveted Senate seat, and three well-known politicians for a time considered making the race. James V. Allred and Martin Dies looked over the list of candidates, found little reason for hope, and never made formal announcements. W. Lee O'Daniel, the incumbent, waited until mid-May before announcing over a network of radio stations that he chose "not to seek reelection." His critics pointed out that only two days previously the Belden poll showed that only fifteen percent of the Texas voters felt that O'Daniel had the capacity to help the state in Washington.

Active and continuous campaigning did not begin in the summer of 1948 until the second week in June, a relatively late date since the primary came in July. John-

Lyndon B. Johnson

son and Stevenson were the most active campaigners. The congressman gained much attention through his use of a helicopter for transportation. He made seven to nine scheduled speeches daily, appeared before fifty to sixty thousand voters a week, and gave a total of 375 scheduled talks; and, whenever from the helicopter he saw a gathering of people, he would swoop down from the sky and conduct an informal rally. The ex-governor drove an aged automobile over the state, buying only five gallons of gasoline at a time, every day trying to shake hands with at least fifty people before breakfast. Stevenson declared that by mid-July he had traveled more than fifty thousand miles and had shaken hands with at least 200,000 people in 211 counties.

Both Peddy and Johnson cited Stevenson's lack of experience in national affairs, said the ex-governor was an isolationist, criticized him for not announcing a platform, derided his endorsement by the labor unions, and denounced his persistent refusal to make clear his stand on the national Taft-Hartley Law (widely publicized as an anti-labor law). Stevenson did not bother to answer these charges and criticisms and never spoke personally against his opponents until very late in the campaign; instead he kept repeating that he was running on his record and said that his life was an open book to the voters.

Johnson kept hammering away at his theme of strong military preparedness; thirty-nine years old during the campaign, he stressed his youth and urged the voters to note his eleven years of experience in Congress. Nevertheless, Stevenson led in the primary, receiving 477,077 votes, while Johnson got 405,617 and Peddy, 237,197. The eight minor candidates had a combined total of 82,403 votes cast for them. Stevenson carried 168 counties, Johnson, 72, and Peddy, 14. Stevenson led in the counties with large cities, Johnson in West Texas and the Rio Grande Valley.

Almost immediately after the results of the July primary were known, both candidates still in the race left for Washington, Johnson to attend a special session of Congress and Stevenson to confer with federal officials about foreign affairs. The congressman stated that he would remain in Washington as long as his presence was needed; the ex-governor said he would return to Texas in a few days. Actually Stevenson spent only two days in the nation's capital. During that time he talked with several senators serving on the Foreign Affairs Committee and with Secretary of Defense James Forrestal; upon his return to Texas the ex-governor declared that the nation's foreign policy was sound and that he would support it. Congressman Johnson wryly remarked that Stevenson had taken the shortest course in foreign relations on record.

The runoff brought little that was new in issues, but differed in that it was bitterly personal. Johnson discarded his helicopter and concentrated his efforts and his time in the large cities, knowing that he had to pick up votes there if he was to win. Stevenson gave up his practice of ignoring charges against himself and started attacking Johnson; he made regularly scheduled speeches and spent less time shaking hands.

During the July primary, very few Texas newspapers had expressed a preference for any candidate, but they were very outspoken during the runoff. The Houston *Post* in August conducted a poll and reported that ten papers in the larger cities had indicated a shift and were supporting Johnson. But the Dallas *News*, which for many years had fought Roosevelt's New Deal, continued blasting Johnson and praising Stevenson. The *News* stated just before election time that the congressman's platform was "all things to all men"; it invited his supporters to explain just what Johnson stood for and said that Johnson was backed by leftist labor groups, corporation lawyers, "J. Frank Dobie, Drew Pearson . . . , and a variety of tycoons."

The Austin *American* in a moderate editorial attempted to defend Johnson and his record; it traced his record in Congress, stressed that he had eleven valuable years of experience on the national scene, and argued that he had acquired during his one year in the navy a knowledge of world conditions which a senator needed. Two paragraphs of the editorial were devoted to a review of the public offices held by Stevenson, ending with the statement that the ex-governor was "regrettably isolated by the limitations of his political background. . . . He has been, with all his public service, denied the training and background to meet the acute problems facing Congress in the world of today. . . ."

Election day came and went, but it was more than two months before Texans knew the identity of the Democratic nominee for the Senate. The outcome was by far the closest in the state's political history. The Texas Election Bureau, an unofficial organization reporting totals for the newspapers, declared at midnight following the voting that Stevenson had polled 470,681 votes, Johnson, 468,787, a difference of less than 1,900. By 5:30 the next afternoon, the count showed Stevenson ahead by only eight votes. During the days that followed, county election officials sent revised reports to Austin, and by September 3 the election bureau estimated that Johnson was ahead of his opponent by seventeen ballots.

The Democratic state convention, scheduled to meet on September 14, had the authority and the obligation to decide which returns were correct and to name the winning candidate. Three times the executive committee canvassed the returns; then they voted. Twenty-eight committee members said that Stevenson had won, and twenty-eight said that Johnson had won. One member of the committee was absent, and only after he arrived was the deadlock broken. The late arrival decided for Johnson, and so the committee reported to the convention that the congressman should be declared the nominee by eighty-seven votes out of almost a million cast. Such was the final vedict of the state convention.

The Stevenson partisans refused to accept this verdict, however, and appealed to the Texas district courts, the higher courts, and all three grades of federal courts. They demanded that the State Senate Investigating Committee, the Federal Bureau of Investigation, and the United States Senate conduct investigations, charging that in several South Texas counties more votes had been cast than there were registered voters. On September 15 federal Judge T. Whitfield Davidson signed a restraining order directing that Lyndon Johnson's name not be printed on the November ballot because of irregularities during the election, and the judge directed that United States commissioners should examine the returns for Duval, Jim Wells, and Zapata counties.

The Johnson forces retaliated, charging that investigations should also be conducted into the returns of several East Texas counties that had given Stevenson large majorities, and they likewise appealed to the courts for a reversal of the Davidson injunction. Justice Hugo Black of the Supreme Court, the administrative officer for the Fifth Circuit, set aside the Davidson injunction, ruling that a federal court had no jurisdiction over state elections.

Stevenson immediately filed a plea with the Supreme Court for a reversal of Black's decision, but on October 5 the highest court in the nation rejected the ex-governor's plea. Stevenson thereupon gave his support to Jack Porter, the Republican candidate opposing Johnson in the general election, but still the congressman won after a stiff fight.

Over the next several months the United States Senate was repeatedly urged to unseat Johnson. A final report in that high body was made on July 26, 1949, stating that the Senate never inquired into the results of a primary election. Thus approximately one year after the primary election, the campaign was over. Still there were many dissatisfied Texans, and some political observers on the national scene were unhappy. *Time,* a weekly news magazine, referred to the Texas senator as "Landslide Lyndon" for several years, deriding the narrowness of his victory.

There was also some excitement in the general election of November 1948 other than the contested Senate seat; President Harry S. Truman was seeking reelection, but owing to his strong demands for civil rights legislation for Negroes, several Southern states had bolted the Democratic party to form the Dixiecrats. Their candidate was J. Strom Thurmond of South Carolina, and they made a strong bid to get the Texas electoral votes. Nevertheless Texas stayed within the Democratic camp, giving its support to Truman.

The gubernatorial contest of 1948 was relatively quiet. Beauford Jester, serving during a time of prosperity, was very popular. He had been able to get the 1947 legislature to vote an increased appropriations bill without asking for new taxes. Hospitals and orphanages had received twice as much money as during the previous year, new eleemosynary institutions were opened, and a host of labor legislation was enacted, including a controversial "right-to-work" law which made it illegal to require that an employee join a labor union. Governor Jester had recommended pay increases for the public school teachers, but the lawmakers had failed to respond; they had, however, sent to the voters a constitutional amendment, subsequently passed, which provided that a special fund be set aside for constructing buildings at fourteen of the state's colleges.

Then came the session of 1949, the longest in state history. Meeting from January 11 to July 6, the Fifty-first Legislature became the first to pass an appropriations bill of more than a billion dollars. The Board for Texas State Hospitals and Special Schools was created and given the task of supervising the state mental hospitals and the schools for handicapped children. And it overhauled the Texas prison system, which had been allowed to become hopelessly inadequate. To care for juvenile offenders, the legislature created the Youth Development Council and put the three reformatories under its administration. A huge appropriation for improvements of the Huntsville prison system was passed, and a modernization program was undertaken to cope with the increased number of offenders.

But the 1949 legislature will best be remembered as the one that passed the Gilmer-Aikin program for modernizing the state school system. The Fiftieth Legislature of 1947 had attempted the task when it passed the Blankenship Act, but Governor Jester announced that he would not sign it because it followed the usual "inadequate, inequitable, and improper method of financing schools." He declared that Texans were paying money to four hundred schools whose average daily attendance was less than ten pupils each, that teacher salaries should be raised to a minimum of $2,700, and that a comprehensive program of reform should be undertaken. The Fiftieth Legislature reacted to the governor's message by establishing a committee to investigate the state's system of public education and to make recommendations to the following legislature.

At the first meeting of the committee, held in the governor's quarters in the capitol in July 1947, the group adopted the name "Gilmer-Aikin Committee," honoring Representative Claud Gilmer of Rocksprings and Senator A. M. Aikin of Paris, both of whom had fought for years for constructive public school legislation. At committee meetings in August and September, sub-committees were appointed to investigate and make special studies. At first the public school teachers of the state were suspicious of the intentions and possibilities of reform, but leading educators interested in reforms were soon convinced that the committee members were honestly seeking a meritorious program. In November 1947 at the meeting of the Texas State Teachers Association at San Antonio, a mild resolution of praise for the work of the Gilmer-Aikin Committee was passed, and gradually the teachers began to cooperate with the legislators.

After an unprecedented amount of work, the committee published its findings and proposals in November 1948; subsequently they were introduced early in the Fifty-first Legislature in three bills designated as emergency measures. The first bill, Senate Bill 115, provided for a reorganization of the public school administration from the local to the state level and called for the creation of an elective State Board of Education and an appointed Commissioner of Education. The second proposal, Senate Bill 116, was the longest and most complicated of the three; it called for the establishment of the "Minimum Foundation Program," designed to provide every child in the state with at least nine months of minimum-quality schooling. It also contained a complicated formula for determining what each local school district should contribute, made a college degree and certain professional training mandatory for all teachers, and set a minimum salary of $3,204 per year for beginning teachers, with specified raises for each year of experience and additional professional training. Senate Bill 117, the third of the proposals, provided for automatic financing for the system, making it unnecessary for the legislature to make appropriations for education from the general revenue fund every two years.

Despite the merits of the Gilmer-Aikin plan, there was strenuous and organized resistance to it. Dr. L. A. Woods of Waco, serving his ninth elective term as State Superintendent of Public Instruction, felt that he would be deprived of his office by the creation of an appointive head of the state school system. Over the years Dr. Woods had made many professional and political friends, and he pressed these people into service in an effort to block the progress of the reform bills.

When the Senate Committee on Education held its first hearing on the three measures, the Senate chamber was filled to overflowing. Sixteen well-informed persons spoke in favor of the legislation, and about the same number argued against the bills. First Assistant State Superintendent of Education T. M. Trimble led the opposition speakers, summarizing all the criticisms that had been offered since November; he declared that the appointment of a Commissioner of Education would be unconstitutional in that it would violate a state contract with Dr. Woods, who had been elected for a two-year term. George Barron, superintendent of the Yoakum schools, objected to the salary schedule based on degrees and experience, charging that such a system would be inequitable; as an example he cited a Negro vocational teacher at Yoakum, the holder of two degrees and a man of long service, who under the proposed system would receive several hundred dollars a year more than the superintendent himself, who had no college degree.

The hearing lasted until well after midnight; then with only one dissenting voice the committee reported the bills favorably. Senator James Taylor, chairman of the committee, reported that he was well pleased with the result and said that he did not foresee any serious controversy when the three measures reached the Senate floor. And he was right, for despite a short filibuster the first measure passed on February 16 by a vote of sixteen to eight; the other two were voted through on March 7 by majorities of twenty-seven to two. All three escaped crippling amendments.

The battle in the House was more prolonged and difficult. Speaker Durwood Manford was an enthusiast for farm-to-market roads and seemed to care little for educational reform. One newspaper insisted that Manford was perfectly willing for the rural population to grow up as "ignoramuses" provided that they could drive to town on paved roads. The backers of the Gilmer-Aikin legislation decided upon a clever bit of "log-rolling"; they became very enthusiastic for better roads. In return, Manford warmed perceptibly to the value and need for school reform.

The House Committee on Education met on March 16 to consider Senate Bills 115, 116, and 117; chairman of the committee was Mrs. Rae Files Still, a member of the Gilmer-Aikin Committee and a spokesman for reform. More than three thousand persons were present when the hearing started at 7 P.M., and several hundred were still on hand when the vote was taken at 5:30 the next morning.

After acrimonious debate, Senate Bill 115 carried by sixteen to five; Bills 116 and 117 by seventeen to two.

Then came the battle on the House floor, one of the longest and bitterest in the history of the Texas legislature. Opponents of the measures used delay tactics; they introduced seemingly endless amendments to kill the measures; they even tried to postpone consideration of the three bills until after the regular session adjourned. But in mid-April when the House adjourned for the week-end, all three measures were still alive. During that week-end Governor Jester stated that school legislation was of "unusual importance" and declined to announce a special session for the purpose of passing or rejecting the Gilmer-Aikin proposals. He directed a statement to the legislators, reminding them that it would soon be time for school boards to elect teachers, set salaries and adopt budgets, and establish tax rates for the new year; what better time, he asked, could the legislators find to pass the pending proposals and better the school system?

The governor's statement was timely and an aid to friends of the Gilmer-Aikin legislation, but opposition continued. Representative Sam Hanna of Dallas stated that he would fight the measures "until Hell freezes over" and held a dinner meeting at an Austin hotel on April 19 for all who felt the way he did. He planned a "walkout" to break a quorum when the first bill came up for a vote, but the plan became well known and friends of the measures were alerted. On April 20 the vote came on House Bill 115; it passed by eighty-six to thirty, with thirty-three absent. A week later House Bill 116 went through easily, 113 to 22, with three present and not voting and ten absent. The final measure, House Bill 117, was passed on April 28 by a vote of 116 to 22, with ten members absent.

Since the House had added several amendments to the

bills, they had to go back to the Senate where two were accepted; the third went to a conference committee where compromises were effected, certain technical errors were eliminated, and a clause was inserted providing for an immediate implementation of the program. Passage of the final measure came on May 31, and all three bills went to the governor for his signature. Through the dedicated efforts of many men, Texans had won a better school system; in fact, many experts called the legislation a "Texas-sized step forward."

Early in July Governor Jester signed his name to the Gilmer-Aikin measures, and they became the law of the state. On July 11, only a few days later, Jester died, and with his passing a new era in Texas politics began: the years of Allan Shivers. And just ahead loomed the fifties, a booming decade of progress and growth.

11

The Fabulous Fifties

SOUNDING MORE LIKE a Chamber of Commerce bulletin than an article in a news magazine, a story in the November 23, 1956, issue of *U.S. News and World Report* asserted, "Texas, an empire within a republic, is shaping up as the new powerhouse of the United States. In the Lone Star State, oil fields are booming. Big, new industries are springing up. Quiet towns are being transformed, almost violently, into large cities with towering skylines."

The article was no exaggeration, however, for during the fifties the economy of Texas surged forward beyond the wildest dreams of even the proverbial tall-tale tellers from the state. In 1955 Texas led every state in the production of oil, petrochemicals, natural gas, carbon black, helium, sulfur, cotton, rice, beef cattle, wool, and mohair. Each year during the decade following the end of World

War II, more than half a billion dollars had been invested in the construction or expansion of industrial facilities. Within the boundaries of the state were ten of the nation's thirty-five fastest-growing cities. Nor was agriculture neglected; in 1957 a six-year drouth finally broke, and the average farm income that year jumped fifty-six percent over the preceding year. To man the machines of industry and to work the farms and ranches, outsiders moved to the state in unprecedented numbers, so that in the mid-fifties one out of four of its residents had been born elsewhere.

No wonder when asked what the future held, Governor Allan Shivers could say, "I think the growth of Texas is unlimited."

All economic indices justified the governor's optimism. In the federal census for manufacturing in 1949, the net value of Texas' industrial products was $1,813,914,000; the same census for 1958 showed a net value of $5,059,428,000 for Texas' manufactured products, a gain in less than a decade of almost two hundred percent. And the workers, as well as the industrialists, benefitted; the total payroll in Texas industries jumped from $922,269,000 in 1949 to $2,294,982,000 in 1958.

One of the major causes for the rapid development of industry in Texas was the abundance of natural resources, especially petroleum. In addition to meeting the needs of its own citizens, the state had sufficient natural gas to supply more than half the nation with the precious fuel through long pipelines stretching eastward to the Atlantic, westward to the Pacific, and northward to the Great Lakes. Not only is oil pumped from the earth in Texas, but it also is converted into usable products within the state. The census of 1958 disclosed that there were 134 refineries in the Lone Star State, employing 43,938 employees, paying them $281,637,000 annually, and producing goods worth

A Petrochemical Plant

$626,596,000 in net value. These petroleum refineries are mainly located at the Gulf port cities, especially along the Houston Ship Channel.

Closely allied to petroleum is the chemical industry. As measured by the annual net value of its products, the chemical industry is the largest, as well as the newest, in the state. In 1958 it brought $1,063,136,000 to Texas. A modern chemical plant is manned by relatively few, but highly trained employees; therefore, despite the fact that the chemical industry was the only segment of the Texas economy to net more than a billion dollars in 1958, it ranked fourth in number of employees. Most of the plants produce petrochemical products; using the hydrocarbons of natural gas and petroleum, they make an almost infinite number of compounds, which in turn are used to produce plastic articles, synthetic rubber, and synthetic fibers. The chemical industry is primarily located near the Gulf coast to take advantage of the relatively inexpensive shipping rates by sea, but there are several plants in the interior of the state, notably in the vicinity of Dallas-Fort Worth, at Odessa in West Texas, around Longview in East Texas, and in the Borger-Pampa area of the Panhandle.

Texas has always ranked low in the production of primary metals, such as iron and steel, because there has never been a mineral source sufficient to support a huge industry. Only two plants of major significance are in the state, that of the Lone Star Steel Company in Morris County and that one located on the Houston Ship Channel and operated by the Sheffield Division of Armco. Aluminum is produced at three Texas plants. There is no bauxite, the aluminum ore, in the state; the mineral is shipped in from Arkansas and foreign countries.

About one half of the 254 counties in Texas have stone and clay deposits that can be commercially exploited, and there are a few glass and sand deposits. Texas pink and gray granite are found in Burnet, Llano, and other counties of the Central Basin. Limestone is quarried and finished for market in Travis and Williamson counties in Central Texas, Jones County in West Texas, and Wise County in North Texas. Brick kilns have been constructed in some thirty counties, and glass is manufactured at Waco and Palestine.

Rounding out the industrial facilities which make use of natural resources in the state for their raw products is the East Texas timbering complex. More than nine hundred plants in the piney woods area turn out lumber, crossties, paper and paper products, and various types of building materials. Trees are now scientifically "farmed," so that within the last decade Texas forests have been growing faster than they have been cut.

Moving into the state in increasing numbers have been industries not related to natural resources. Among this group would be included the plants manufacturing scientific and technical instruments and components, such as the transistors and electronic devices fashioned by Texas Instruments at Dallas; there are the makers of heavy equipment, such as cotton gins, oil field and construction machinery, farm implements, and general industrial equipment; Ford Motor Company has plants at Houston and Dallas where automobiles are assembled and General Motors maintains a similar establishment at Arlington; and there are several manufacturers of aircraft, such as Chance-Vought, which took over the North American plant at Grand Prairie, Convair, successor to the war-time Consolidated Aircraft plant at Fort Worth, Bell Helicopter at Hurst, and Temco at Grand Prairie, Garland, and Greenville. Unfortunately, the shipbuilding yards that flourished during World War II have declined in importance.

The third type of industrial development within recent years has been that related to the processing of farm and ranch products. Canneries and freezing plants to prepare food for market numbered 1,936 in 1958. Textile mills have not been built at the rate many Texans had hoped, but progress has been steady; in 1958 there were seventy-six such establishments, including thirty cotton mills and three using wool. From the hides of cattle come the raw material for leather, and since Texas is the leading cattle-producing state in the nation it is only natural that shoes, boots, and saddles should be made in Texas. Several Texas bootmakers or companies have become famous throughout the West, including Tony Lima, Nocona, and Justin.

And these industries are but a few of the many within the state. There are furniture makers, apparel factories, printing establishments, and other industries related to those already named. Texas during World War II started down the road to industrialization, and by the fifties more people were living in the cities, more citizens were making their living in factories, than had been dreamed possible just a few short decades before. At the turn of the twentieth century, most Texans felt their state was destined to remain an area devoted to farming and ranching; by 1960 agriculture was still a mainstay of the economy, but the farms and ranches were far behind the factories in value of goods produced.

Politics, however, still moved in the usual channels, still was conducted according to the Constitution of 1876 and the Terrell Election Law, and still engendered a great deal of heat and color.

Upon the death of Beauford Jester in July 1949, the

lieutenant governor, Allan Shivers, had succeeded to the chief executive's office. The new governor had served for ten years in the state Senate before becoming lieutenant governor; thus he had considerable experience in the ways of Texas politics.

Within a short time after he came to office, Shivers found it necessary to call a special session of the legislature. The lawmakers had been so busy passing the controversial school legislation in 1949 that they had not adequately seen to the financial needs of the state. Not only did Shivers get the appropriation he wanted from the special session, but he got increased taxes to finance the expenditures as well.

In the July primary of 1950, Texans were diverted somewhat from the election by the Korean War, which had begun only a month earlier. Shivers proved himself an able campaigner and won easily over six opponents. But his first elective term as chief executive was no easy one, for the 1951 legislative session had before it several controversial measures. Nevertheless, the governor managed to get most of his campaign promises enacted into law. And for the first time in thirty years the state was redistricted for legislative purposes, giving West Texas and the larger cities additional representation; new taxes were levied, and several existing ones were raised; governmental employees were given pay raises, long overdue and badly needed; and an automobile-inspection law was passed requiring a safety inspection of all vehicles driven on the public roads.

Then came the memorable election of 1952, of interest not only because of the contest for governor and a United States Senate seat, but for the fight to get the state's electoral college votes for President. Several changes, amounting to a political revolution, occurred that year;

for the first time since 1928, Texas was carried by a Republican presidential candidate, and, more astonishing, the leading Democratic politicians within the state, including the governor, supported the Republican party. The causes of this remarkable shift lay in Washington and in the personalities of the contenders for the presidency.

When Harry S. Truman became President in April 1945, he declared that he would continue Roosevelt's policies, and for a short time his leadership was approved by most people, including Texans. But within two years, the situation changed. The original New Deal workers left the government and were replaced by men of a different type—machine politicians, small-town lawyers, and business men with little experience in government. Especially mistaken were Truman's appointments to departments dealing with domestic affairs where several administrators took advantage of their financial opportunities. Standards of honesty in the lower brackets of some departments, notably the Bureau of Internal Revenue, declined to such an extent that they approximated those of the Grant and Harding years. Actual bribery and theft were seldom proven, but a laxity in ethics was very apparent in Washington; in the newspapers there were many articles devoted to such subjects as "five-percenters," gifts of deep freezes, mink coats, and loans showered upon persons with influence who could deliver special privileges and lucrative government contracts.

Governor Shivers, announcing for reelection in January 1952, declared: "A change must occur in the national trend, not alone for the welfare of Texas citizens but for the benefit of the nation and the world. . . . " He was opposed by Ralph W. Yarborough, a former district judge and an Austin lawyer who entered the race as a self-announced "liberal-conservative."

In the Senate race, Attorney General Price Daniel declared he would seek the post, and in his opening address severely attacked the Truman administration, charging it with graft, greed, extravagance, and socialism. His opponent in the contest for the seat held for twenty-four years by Tom Connally, who did not seek reelection in 1952, was Congressman Lindley Beckworth of Gladewater. Beckworth, largely unknown outside his East Texas district, was a pro-administration Democrat.

Shivers and Daniel banded together during the campaign preceding the July primary and ran on similar platforms. A special issue was the Texas claim to the tidelands, a ten-mile strip extending outward from the coast and rich in oil deposits. The tidelands had become an issue in 1945 when the United States government announced that Texas could legally claim only three miles out. The fight for this valuable strip had continued in court and the legislative halls of Congress, with Price Daniel, attorney general since 1947, leading much of the battle. Both Shivers and Daniel declared they would fight the "tidelands grab" by the federal government; they hammered away at the issues of graft and corruption in high places, at "Trumanism," at the "mess in Washington," at the dangers of inflation, and at the continued encroachment of the federal government upon the state's powers.

Since the two major candidates spoke so much about national affairs, the voters of the state naturally became concerned about them and kept a careful watch on the national phases of the two races. The Texas delegation to the Democratic national convention favored the nomination of Senator Richard Russell of Georgia for President, but it had to submit to the leadership and sponsorship of Truman in the nomination of Governor Adlai Stevenson of Illinois, a liberal millionaire. Shivers and Daniel reacted to this event by announcing that they favored the "Texas Democratic Party" and would not support the national Democratic party under the Truman leadership.

As a result of the Shivers-Daniel pronouncement, Texans kept a keen eye on the Republican national convention, and many were delighted when General Dwight D. Eisenhower, a native of Texas who grew up in Kansas, was nominated. The platform pledged a general cleaning of the level of government and criticized the Democrats for practically every bit of legislation of the past twenty years.

The Democratic primary in Texas, held July 26, was conducted while the Texas delegation was attending the national party convention in Chicago and was widely regarded as a preferential primary in the presidential contest. Congressman Beckworth, thought of by many Texans as a representative of the Truman administration and the "Tidelands Steal," was decisively defeated in the Senate race; he received 285,842 votes, Daniel, 940,770. Judge Yarborough was likewise known as a "loyal" Democrat and a supporter of the Truman Fair Deal, and he suffered the same fate as Beckworth. Shivers polled 833,861 votes, Yarborough, 488,345. The result of the Texas primary greatly heartened the Republicans across the nation and made them feel that they might carry the Lone Star State for their nominee.

Naturally Texans were concerned about the attitudes of the two presidential candidates toward the tidelands. Eisenhower had already declared that he supported the Texas position; he said he felt that federal ownership of land was "calculated to bring about steady progress toward centralized ownership and control, a trend that I have bitterly opposed." Governor Shivers approached Adlai Stevenson for a statement; the Democratic nominee replied with praise for a recent Supreme Court decision denying state control of the tidelands. Shivers thereupon announced that he could not support the Democratic candidate in the presidential race.

Following the quiet primary on August 23, the state's voters turned their attention to the Democratic state convention to be held in Amarillo on September 9. Loyal Democrats insisted that they would organize and control the convention and carry the state for Stevenson in November. But the "Eisenhower Democrats," as well as the Republicans, disagreed. Daniel said in a radio address on September 1 that Texans "must choose between the national Democratic party and the Democratic party of Texas." Governor Shivers announced that he would recommend voting a "split ticket"; Texans should choose Eisenhower for President, then switch to the Democratic column and vote for the party's state nominees.

The state Democratic convention adopted the Shivers' policy. The newspapers reported that the convention "reluctantly put Adlai Stevenson on its ballot, then urged that every Democrat in Texas should vote and work for Dwight D. Eisenhower for President."

In the fall of the year both candidates for President and both candidates for Vice-President spoke in Texas; even President Truman made a "whistle stop" tour recommending the election of Stevenson. Democrats used such slogans as "You never had it so good" and "Don't let them take it away," but there were thousands of citizens over the nation who spoke freely of the "mess in Washington" and urged that 1952 was "time for a change."

Governor Allan Shivers headed a "Democrats for Eisenhower" group and frequently referred to the 1952 election as a "year of decision." Texans widely believed the charge made in the Dallas *News* that the major issue was "Texas' historical right to its own lands." Another *News* editorial asserted, "A vote for Stevenson is a vote for the corruption, the graft, the debt, the inefficiency, and the scandals of the Truman administration, because, says Harry Truman, 'Stevenson is running on my record. He has nothing else to run on. This is it.' "

To the astonishment of all observers, there were more than two million votes cast in the general election of November 1952; the figure represented more than a seventy-two percent increase over the highest total ever compiled in a general election. Eisenhower received the vote of 1,102,878 Texans; Stevenson, 970,128. Over the nation as a whole, the Republican candidate led by more than six and one-half million, with almost sixty-two million ballots being cast.

And the Eisenhower administration proved quite popular when it got into office. The President kept his word by asking Congress to pass a special law giving Texas the right to its tidelands, and this was done. Partly as a result of this and partly because they felt his administration compared so favorably to the Truman years that preceded it, Texans in 1956 again voted Republican. The same two candidates sought the office, this time Eisenhower running on his record and Stevenson criticizing it. The Texas result was Eisenhower, 1,080,619; Stevenson, 859,958.

In 1954 Shivers asked the voters of the state to give him an unprecedented third term. The 1953 legislature had faced the usual problem of finding additional tax revenues to pay for the increased state services which Texans were coming to take for granted. A raise for school teachers had failed to carry, but eleven amendments to the constitution had been sent to the voters. All of them were subsequently accepted, and included such measures as higher legislative salaries, jury service for women, and the vote for Texans in the armed forces. The governor campaigned on the need for getting the rest of his program enacted into law. His chief opponent again was Judge Ralph W. Yarborough, and in the runoff the vote was Shivers, 775,088; Yarborough, 683,132. In that same election Lyndon Johnson won a second term in the United States Senate, this time by a less embarrassing margin.

In 1955 when the legislature met, the state faced a grave financial crisis—one hundred million dollars in new revenue was desperately needed. Cries for a sales tax or an income tax filled the air, but once again the lawmakers avoided these issues by raising existing taxes. Texans suddenly found that gasoline, cigarettes, and alcoholic beverages cost slightly more, and the franchise tax paid by corporations reached a new high. To supervise the courses and degrees offered at the state colleges and universities, the legislature created the Commission on Higher Education. And because of the record-breaking number of failures among insurance companies, the 1955 session devoted much time to the enactment of a new insurance code.

Shivers' third term was not a happy one because of a scandal in the veterans' land program. In gratitude for the services of its fighting men during World War II, the state had voted a bond issue of one hundred million dollars, the funds to be used to purchase land for resale as farms to veterans at very favorable terms. A Veterans' Land Board supervised the program; its members consisted of the governor, the attorney general, and the commissioner of the land office. Early in 1956 certain irregularities came to light, leading to investigations by a grand jury and by senate and house committees. A number of officials, including Bascom Giles, the commissioner of the land office, were sentenced to prison as a result of the investigations.

In the Democratic primary in 1956 Senator Price Daniel declared that he would seek the gubernatorial nomination. His major opponent was Ralph Yarborough, who was making his third try for the office. Yarborough, a liberal, received the support of labor groups, regular Democrats who had not bolted the party in 1952, and racial minority groups. The judge conducted a spirited campaign, charging that Daniel, along with the governor and Attorney General John Ben Shepperd, had been lax in administering the veterans' land funds.

Four other candidates entered the contest, including former Governor W. Lee O'Daniel and J. Evetts Haley, the conservative West Texas rancher and historian. Charges and counter-charges, hot tempers, and the excitement of former years were matched by the 1956 spectacle, but it was the moderately conservative Price Daniel who emerged as the victor. In the runoff with Judge Yarborough, the senator polled 698,001 votes; the judge received 694,830.

In January 1957 Daniel took office, replacing Shivers who had served for seven and one-half years, the longest administration of any chief executive since Texas became a state. Almost immediately, Daniel was swept up in the turmoil of politics, for the 1957 legislature had a very stormy session. Investigations revealed that several legislators were on retainer fees from several large corporations with vested interests to protect. One representative was convicted of accepting a bribe and was sentenced to a term in the state penitentiary. A measure to control the lobbyists failed, despite the work of the governor to secure its passage. With education, however, the lawmakers proved very generous. Teachers' salaries were raised by $399, and colleges were given increased support through a doubling of tuition. The lawmakers also tightened the laws regulating insurance companies, and a State Board of Water Development was created in an effort to get dams built across the state in order to avoid the dire results of another drouth.

A special election held in the spring of 1957 to fill the senate seat vacated by Governor Price Daniel finally allowed Ralph Yarborough to win an important voice in Texas politics. He defeated Dallas millionaire businessman William Blakely for the office.

As was expected by everyone, Price Daniel announced in 1958 that he would seek a second term. His most important opponent was Henry B. Gonzales, state senator from San Antonio, who was known as a liberal. Daniel easily won.

Again in 1959 the most important task facing the legislature was finding sufficient funds to run the state for the next biennium. Nothing positive was accomplished during the regular session, and the governor felt compelled to call three special sessions before a compromise tax measure was passed, raising most of the needed revenue. An appropriations bill was passed only a few days before the August 31 deadline when the old appropriations expired. In addition, more water laws were passed, and the insurance code was further revised.

When the spring of 1960 arrived, the usual political flowers began to sprout. Daniel followed the precedent established by Allan Shivers and asked that the voters return him for a third term. The most pressing issue of the race was state finances, and after a bitter struggle with Jack Cox of Breckenridge, who advocated a sales tax, Governor Daniel received the Democratic nomination for a third term. In the general election he faced stiff Republican opposition and found it necessary to campaign more than any Democratic nominee in recent history. Nevertheless, he was elected, as Texans returned to the Democratic fold in national politics by giving their electoral votes to John F. Kennedy. Republican nominee Richard M. Nixon lost by only sixty thousand out of approximately two million ballots cast, however, leading to speculation that Texas could never again be taken for granted as part of the solidly Democratic South. Perhaps the reason Kennedy won in Texas, at least according to some political experts, was because his vice-presidential running mate was Lyndon B. Johnson.

As the Lone Star State entered the "Soaring Sixties," many changes were evident, but the future looked very bright. Industrialization was proceeding at a rapid pace, farm and ranch incomes were at record levels, two-party politics seemed a certainty, college enrollments and the number of students in the public schools stood at an all-time high, and the population passed the ten million mark. And, almost four and one-half centuries after the first Spanish explorer viewed the coastline of Texas, another exploratory party was preparing to depart, this time from the Lone State State, but again toward the unknown. The National Aeronautics and Space Administration, the federal agency charged with overseeing the United States effort to reach the moon, announced that it would locate at Houston.

Epilogue

ANOTHER CHAPTER was beginning in the story of Texas, truly a chronicle of greatness. Few, however, expected the era to begin on notes so discordant as declining political influence at the national level, a rush of scandals, and a presidential assassination in Texas.

During the twentieth century, Lone Star statesmen had made many contributions to the nation's political development—men such as Edward M. House, John Nance Garner, and Sam Rayburn. Yet following the election of 1960 Texans seemed forever destined to be consultants and legislators rather than chief executives. Favorite sons of Texas appeared to be tainted by prejudices against Southerners, whatever their pretensions of being Southwesterners or Westerners rather than sons of the Confederacy. Certainly Lyndon Johnson's failure to attain the Democratic nomination in San Francisco in 1960 showed the lack of national enthusiasm for a Texas aspirant. Moreover, Johnson's unsuccessful bid signalled the start of a series of developments that threatened to end the influence wielded by Texans at the national level.

As majority leader in the United State Senate, Johnson frequently had been compared to Henry Clay for his ability to "get things done." But as Vice-President his role in national affairs was greatly diminished. Then in 1961 cancer claimed Speaker of the House Sam Rayburn, and Texas lost another strong voice in Washington. The following year John Connally resigned as secretary of the navy, a post he had obtained in the Kennedy administration through Johnson's efforts. Connally returned to the

Lone Star State to campaign for and win the governorship, but this meant still another reduction of Texans in responsible federal positions in Washington.

Then came the agricultural scandals of Pecos promoter Billy Sol Estes, who was convicted of manipulating cotton acreage allotments to his own advantage and of mortgaging fertilizer tanks that existed only on paper. Estes threatened to implicate certain other high-ranking politicians who had accepted campaign gifts from him. And, finally, there were the questionable activities of Bobby Baker, a one-time protegé of Johnson; the Baker scandal cast a cloud on the career of the Vice-President—as did charges that the Johnson fortune had been accumulated through high-handed business practices and the use of government influence to keep a nearly monopolistic television franchise in Austin.

As the year 1963 advanced toward autumn, rumors persisted that Johnson would be dropped from the national Democratic ticket in 1964. He had become a political liability. Texas statesmen had never faced a more perplexing future—and Texas Democrats were feuding among themselves. The majority party in the Lone Star State was split into liberal and conservative factions, the liberals led by Senator Ralph Yarborough and the conservatives by Governor John Connally. Seemingly the two factions could not agree, and Johnson persuaded President Kennedy to make a speaking tour through the state. At the same time Kennedy could work to heal the split in order to keep Texas' electoral votes securely in the Democratic column in 1964.

The tour ended in a tragedy of international proportions. On November 22, 1963, as the President motored into Dallas from the airport, two shots were fired from a fifth-floor window of the Texas School Book Depository

Building in Dallas—both bullets struck the President, and one of them seriously wounded Governor John Connally. Lee Harvey Oswald, the accused killer, was in turn shot himself two days later by Jack Ruby, a Dallas nightclub operator, in a bizarre episode watched by millions of Americans; television cameras had caught and recorded the deed.

Immediately following the assassination of President Kennedy, Lyndon Johnson took the oath of office in Air Force One at Love Field in Dallas. The widowed Jacqueline Kennedy was a witness, and the slain President was a passenger on the return flight to Washington. Through three days of numbed sadness, the body of the late President moved in solemn procession toward its final resting place in Arlington National Cemetery.

Into the political vacuum left by the assassination stepped the tall, politically prudent Texan, Lyndon Johnson. Congress and the nation agreed with him when he tearfully declared that he "would give all that I own" not to have been shackled with the duties of chief executive under such dreadful circumstances. Yet all breathed a relieved sigh that a person of Johnson's caliber and stature had succeeded to the White House. His reputation as a skilled legislator and experienced statesman was reassuring.

Johnson's immediate post-assassination popularity was phenomenal, and the disquieting rumors of a few weeks before were forgotten in the days and weeks that followed. Leaders throughout the world hurried to confer with him, just as did congressmen and governors of the various states. People everywhere gladly recalled the statement made in 1960 by John Kennedy—that if anything should happen to him, he knew of no man he would prefer to have succeed him than Johnson.

In his drawling Texas manner, Johnson reassured the nation and the world of the continuation of Kennedy's policies, and soon the new President had attracted a fantastic following. Newsmen reported the President's impromptu two-mile-hike press conferences; security guards moaned as the commander in chief ignored their pleas and ordered the White House gates thrown open to admiring sidewalk visitors; and friends and diplomats converged gleefully at the LBJ ranch in Texas for brisk horseback rides and tasty barbecues in a relaxed and informal atmosphere.

So captivating was Johnson's manner that by the eve of the 1964 Democratic convention, the presidential nomination, usually a spirited contest, obviously belonged to the Texan in the White House. And in the election that followed, the sting of Republican criticism was dissipated by fights within the Republicans' own ranks. The Republicans could not agree among themselves to support their nominee, Barry M. Goldwater, a conservative Arizona senator. On election day, Johnson topped his opponent by the largest percentage of popular votes in over a century. A Texan—the first—had been elected to the White House in his own right.

It is impossible at this writing to assess the "Johnson years." But clearly a new era has dawned for the state and the nation. If he carries out his promise of a "Great Society," Johnson may well lead the United States into one of its brightest and most hopeful periods. Whatever the outcome of his years in office, however, it is evident that the President has brought a deeper respect for Texas-flavored Western culture, and he has brought a note of informality to our nation's capital. For the present, at least, the eyes of the nation and the world are upon Texas, and a Texan guides the destinies of enlightened mankind.

Point of View

THE SERIOUS STUDENT of the modern era of Texas history quickly discovers that there have been relatively few usable published works on this period. Perhaps the recent past is still so close that it is difficult to gain the necessary perspective; certainly many of the materials commonly used to write such histories are as yet unavailable. Newspapers, magazines, and government documents will have to serve until letters, diaries, private papers, and reminiscences become available. And the problem of materials is further compounded by the fact that as yet there have been few monographs, biographies, or other studies in depth.

The best works on the modern period include Ralph Steen's *Twentieth Century Texas: an Economic and Social History* (Austin, 1942) and S. S. McKay's *Texas Politics, 1906-1944* (Lubbock, 1952). F. C. Adams, ed., *Texas Democracy* (4 vols., Austin, 1937) is of limited use in the study of politics.

Biographies which have already appeared and are helpful include Sam Acheson's *Joe Bailey, the Last Democrat* (New York, 1932); and Emma M. Shirley's *The Administration of Pat M. Neff, Governor of Texas, 1921-1925*, Baylor University Bulletin, Vol. XLI, No. 4, 1938.

For the controversial subject of Texas politics, there are many newspaper and magazine articles which give pertinent facts and interesting insights. Serious works include S. S. McKay's three pioneering works, *Texas Politics, 1906-1944* (Lubbock, 1952); *W. Lee O'Daniel and Texas Politics, 1938-1942* (Lubbock, 1944); and *Texas and the Fair Deal, 1945-1952* (San Antonio, 1954). The biographies listed above contain many references to politics, and D. B. Hardeman's "Shivers of Texas: a Tragedy in Three Acts," *Harpers,* November 1956, is excellent for the early and middle fifties.

Those seeking information on the subject of economics should consult numerous state and federal government publications. Especially valuable are the annual reports of the State Commissioner of Agriculture. Publications of the Works Progress Administration and the Office of Old Age and Survivors Insurance (Social Security) are good federal sources for facts about Texas during the depression. Riley E. Baker's "Water Development as an Important Factor in the Utilization of the High Plains," *Southwestern Social Science Quarterly,* XXVI, contains a fine account of a pivotal element in the boom in West Texas agriculture; a handy reference on the petroleum industry is Carl Coke Rister's book, *Oil! Titan of the Southwest* (Norman, Okla., 1949). Ernest R. Bartley's study, *The Tidelands Oil Controversy* (Austin, 1953), tells the story of the valuable offshore lands for which Texans fought the federal government.

Three other studies are more than worthy of mention. No bibliography, however selective, should be offered without a reference to the Texas Rangers, the famous group which was used in so many instances in twentieth century Texas to insure law and order. The study of this organization is Walter Prescott Webb's *The Texas Rangers* (Boston and New York, 1935). For the settlement of West Texas, the name of William Curry Holden stands far ahead of others who have studied this development; his work, *Alkali Trails* (Dallas, 1930), has already become a classic. And S. A. MacCorkle's "The Pardoning Power in Texas," *Southwestern Social Science Quarterly,* XV, is an excellent examination of a topic which stirred Texans deeply in the twenties and thirties.

Walter P. Webb and H. Bailey Carroll, ed., *The Handbook of Texas* (Austin, 1953) is of limited use in the study of this period. Biographical sketches are included only for people who died prior to the late 1940's, and general coverage stops at about that time. *The Texas Almanac,* published biennially, provides a wealth of statistical data on Texas during the twentieth century.

A bibliography, no matter what its pretensions, is never complete. This one makes no such boast. Instead, it is intended as a guide for those who wish to do further reading and a starting point for those who wish to do serious research.

Index

Beckworth, Lindley, election of 1952, 217-218
Belden, Joe (*see* Belden Poll)
Belden Poll: election of 1946, 195; election of 1948, 197; taxation, 167
Bell, C. K., prohibition movement, 24
Bell County, 42, 46, 147
Bell helicopter, 213
Belton, Texas, 147, 149; J. E. Ferguson at, 42-43
Big Lake Field, opened, 100
Big Spring, Texas, influence of oil on, 102-103
Biggers, Don Hampton, investigation of highway frauds, 107
Black, Hugo, election of 1948, 201
Blakely, William, election of 1957, 223
Blankenship Act, 203
Board of Pardons and Paroles: disbanded, 89; reestablished, 150
Borger, A. P., town built by, 102
Borger, Texas: chemical plant at, 212; growth of, 102; lawlessness at, 102
Borger Field, opened, 101
Bosque County, 121
Breakwater (ship), use of diesel fuel, 9
Breckenridge, Texas, 223
Brenham, Texas, 123, 130; prejudice in during World War I, 72-73
Brooks, M. M., prohibition movement, 24
Brooks, Pierce P., election of 1936, 145-149
Brooks Field: World War I aviation, 63; World War II aviation, 185
Bryan, William Jennings, 18, 26, 36, 45
Bryan *Daily Eagle,* quoted, 46, 73
Buffalo, Texas, 159
Burkburnett Field, opened, 100
Burkett, Joe, support of J. E. Ferguson, 87-88

Burleson, Albert Sidney, 34, 35; career of, 38
Burnet County, 213
Burt Oil Company, refinery built by, 11
Business and commerce (*see* Industry and names of individual companies)
Butte, George C., election of 1924, 91-92

California, 42, 188
Call Field, World War I aviation, 63
Camp Bowie, 62
Camp Dick, World War I aviation, 63
Camp Leon Springs, 62
Camp Logan, 62
Camp McArthur, 62
Camp Travis, 62
Campbell, Thomas M., 27; election of 1906, 24; election of 1910, 32; election of 1914, 45; prohibition movement, 24-26
Canyon, Texas, 136
Carroll, H. Bailey, 231
Carson County, 101
Carswell Field, World War II aviation, 185-186
Cattle and cattle industry (*see* Ranching)
Chance-Vought, 213
Chemical industry, growth of, 212
Chicago, Illinois, 218
Childress, Texas, 158
Citrus industry, introduction in Rio Grande Valley, 98
Civilian Conservation Corps, 120
Cleveland, Grover, 18, 37
Coleman, Texas, 123
Colleges (*see* individual colleges)
Colorado, 42
Colorado City, Texas, 158; influence of oil on, 102-103
Colquitt, Oscar B., 43, 140; election of 1906, 24; election of

1910, 25, 32; quoted on Texas politics, 17
Columbia University, 40
Commerce (*see* Industry, Banks, and names of individual companies)
Commerce, Texas, 136
Commissioner of Education, office established, 204-208
Committee To Defend America by Aiding the Allies, 183
Congressional Record, quoted, 81
Connally, John, 225-226, 227
Connally, Tom, elected U. S. senator, 114
Connecticut, 34
Consolidated Aircraft Corporation, 186-187
Constitution (Texas), efforts to write a new one, 51-52, 70, 86-87
Controversy at the University of Texas, 1944-1945, noted, 192
Convair, 213
"Coolidge Prosperity," 117
Cornell University, 35
Corpus Christi, Texas, as naval air training center in World War II, 186
Corsicana, Texas: early oil production at, 3, 9; refinery at, 11, 14
Cotton: farming in West Texas, 96; during Great Depression, 127-128; during World War II, 187
Cox, Jack, election of 1960, 223-224
Cox, James M., 81
Crane, M. M.: election of 1914, 45; election of 1924, 91; suit against Waters-Pierce Oil Company, 21
Crane County, oil discovered in, 102
Crime (*see* Lawlessness)
Cuero, Texas, 130
Culberson, Charles Allen, 35; election of 1922, 85-86; life of, 33-34

Cullinan, J. S.: refinery at Corsicana built by, 11; Texas Company organized by, 14-15
Cumberland University, 18
Curtis Standard JN4D Military Tractor, World War I aviation, 63

Daingerfield, Texas, steel mill at, 187
Dallam County, surveyed for oil, 100
Dallas, Texas, industry at, 213
Dallas *News,* 52, 171, 177; election of 1924, 91; election of 1930, 122; election of 1940, 165; election of 1942, 179-180; election of 1948, 199-200; election of 1952, 219-220; special legislative session of 1937, 151
Dallas *Times-Herald,* election of 1938, 158
Daniel, Price: election of 1952, 217-218; election of 1956, 222; election of 1958, 223; election of 1960, 223-224; as governor, 222-223
Davidson, Lynch, election of 1922, 88-90
Davidson, R. V., 43; opposition to J. W. Bailey, 19; Waters-Pierce suit, 21-22
Davidson, T. Whitfield, 87-88; election of 1922, 88-90; election of 1948, 201
Davis, "Cyclone," in prohibition movement, 26
Dealey, Samuel D., World War II, 184
Democratic National Convention: of 1908, 22-23, 43; of 1912, 36; of 1928, 112-113; of 1936, 146; of 1952, 215, 217; of 1964, 228
Democratic Party (*see also* Elections), 27, 34, 35, 36, 44, 59, 112, 113, 200, 218, 226
Democratic State Executive Committee, 66, 120, 200, 219

Ferguson, Miriam A., 142-143, 151; election of 1924, 88-92; election of 1926, 108-111; election of 1930, 120-125; election of 1932, 128-132; election of 1934, 139; election of 1940, 163-166; election of 1946, 194; governor, 104-108, 139; Ku Klux Klan ended by, 92, 105; marriage to J. E. Ferguson, 42

Ferguson Forum (Temple): election of 1918, 66-70; establishment of, 54-55; highway frauds, 106-107

"56 Club," 162, 165, 168

Fifty-sixth Cavalry, in World War II, 184

First Cavalry Division, in World War II, 184

Fischer, F. W., election of 1936, 145-149

Florida, 184

Food Administration, World War I, 65

Ford Motor Company, plant in Texas built by, 213

Forrestal, James, 199

Fort Bliss, 62

Fort Sam Houston, 62

Fort Worth, Texas: industry at, 186-187, 213; O'Daniel at, 152-155; World War II aviation, 185-186

Fort Worth *Star-Telegram:* election of 1938, 156-157; election of 1942, 179; quoted on J. E. Ferguson, 88

Fourth Army, trained in Texas, 184-185

Gainesville, Texas, 79, 158; Joe Bailey at, 18, 34

Galey, John H.: Gulf Oil Corporation organized by, 13-14; refinery built by, 11

Galveston, Texas, 73

Galveston, Harrisburg and San Antonio Railroad, diesel locomotives used by, 9

Garland, Texas, 186, 213

Garner, John Nance, 146, 225; election of 1941, 169-171

Gas production (*see* Oil and Gas industry)

Gates, John W., 15

General Motors, plants built in Texas, 213

Georgetown, Texas, 158

Georgia, 217; Ku Klux Klan organized in, 76

German-Americans: election of 1918, 68-70; during World War I, 72-74; during World War II, 186

Giles, Bascom, 222

Gilmer, Claud, educational reforms by, 204-208

Gilmer-Aikin Committee, meetings of, 204-205

Gilmer-Aikin law, 204-208

Gladewater, Texas, 217

Gladys City Oil, Gas and Manufacturing Company, organized, 3

Glenn Pool, oil discovered at, 13

Goldwater, Barry M., 228

Gonzales, Texas, 10

Gould, Charles N., Panhandle oil fields opened by, 100-101

Grand Prairie, Texas, 213; as naval air training center in World War II, 186

Graves, Harry N., 135-136

Graves Bill, 136

Graves-Woodruff Reorganization Bill (*see* Griffinhagen Report)

Gray County, oil discovered in, 101

Great Depression, 116; Allred works to end, 143-151; beginning of, 117-118; effect of, 118-120; election of 1930, 120-125; election of 1932, 128-132; election of 1934, 138-142; end of, 186; Mrs. Ferguson works to end, 132-137; Sterling works to end, 125-128

"Great Society," 228

Greenville, Texas, 161, 213

Gregory, Thomas Watt, 34; career of, 38-39

Griffinhagen and Associates, report of, 135

Griffinhagen Report: election of 1934, 140; rejected by legislature, 135-136

Guadalupe Peak, 104

Guffey, James M., refinery built by, 11

Gulf, Colorado and Santa Fe Railroad, use of diesel locomotives, 9

Gulf Oil Corporation, organized, 13-14

Haley, J. Evetts: election of 1956, 222; University of Texas controversy, 192

Halsey, Mark, Jr., 169

Halsey Resolution, 169, 172

Hamil, Al, 2-5

Hamilton, James, 76-77

Hanna, Sam, opposition to Gilmer-Aikin plan, 207

Hardeman, D. B., 230

Hardin, Carl, 135

Harper *Herald*, quoted on election of 1940, 166

Harvard University, 39

Hawaii, 182

Henry, Robert L., support of by J. E. Ferguson, 42

Hester, George C., 166-167

Hicks, Robert, quoted on W. L. O'Daniel, 156

Higgins, Patillo, oil explorations of, 3

High Plains: agriculture on, 95-96; irrigation on, 93-96; oil and gas found on, 100-101; ranching on, 96

Highway Patrol, part of Department of Public Safety, 144

Highways: construction of, 98-99; during Ferguson administration, 106-109; issue in election of 1930, 121-124; issue in election of 1932, 129-131

Hill, Robert T., on use of oil, 10

Hillbilly Flour, marketed by W. L. O'Daniel, 153

Hillsboro, Texas, 9, 125

Hines, Harry, election of 1940, 163-166

Hobby, Oveta Culp, 71, 184

Hobby, William Pettus: election of 1918, 66-70; election of 1920, 79-80; election of 1924, 92; election of 1946, 194; governor, 59-66, 70-71; impeachment of J. E. Ferguson, 56-57, 59-60; life of, 57-60, 71; World War I, 60-66

Hodges, Tom, 76-77

Hoffman Construction Company, sued by State of Texas, 107

Hogg, James Stephen, 35, 170; death of, 32-33; investment in Texas Company, 14-15

Hogg, Mike, election of 1930, 125

Holden, William Curry, 230

Hoover, Herbert, 122, 132, 136; election of 1928, 114; during Great Depression, 117-119; during World War I, 65

Horse racing, legalized, 134

House, Boyce, description of oil speculation at Beaumont, 6-7

House, Edward Mandell, 225; career of, 33-35

Houston, Andrew Jackson, as U. S. senator, 170

Houston, David Franklin, 34, 45; career of, 39-40

Houston, Sam, praised by W. L. O'Daniel, 169-170

Houston: air training center in World War II, 185; Democratic National Convention at, 112-113; industry at, 123, 187; W. P. Hobby's career in, 58

Houston and Texas Central Railroad, use of diesel locomotives, 9

Houston *Chronicle:* election of 1930, 122; stand on sales tax, 133

Houston *Post,* 58, 71; election of

1914, 45; election of 1934, 141; election of 1948, 199; sales tax, 133

Houston *Post-Dispatch*, election of 1924, 92; election of 1930, 122

Huff, Leon, campaigner for W. L. O'Daniel, 159

Hughes, Maury, election of 1934, 139-141

Hughes Springs, Texas, 48

Humble, Texas, discovery of oil at, 11-12

Humble Oil and Refining Company, 121, 123; founded, 15

Hunter, Tom, 131-132; election of 1932, 129-130; election of 1934, 139-142; election of 1936, 145-149; election of 1938, 157-159

Huntsville, Texas, 115, 122

Hurst, Texas, 213

Hutchinson County, oil discovered in, 101

Illinois, 187, 218

Income tax (*see also* Taxes): advocated for state, 28, 126, 133-134, 144, 160

Industry (*see also* names of individual companies, Refineries, Pipelines, and Oil and Gas industry): during the 1920's, 99-100; during the Great Depression, 118; during World War II, 186-187; in post-World War II period, 209-214

Inflation, during World War I, 65

Inheritance tax (*see also* Taxes), 28-29

Insurance companies, laws regulating, 29

International Wire Communication Conference, 38

Invisible Empire (*see* Ku Klux Klan)

Iowa, 187

Irrigation: in Rio Grande Valley, 98; on High Plains, 93-96; powered by diesel, 10

J. M. Guffey Petroleum Company (*see* Gulf Oil Corporation)

Jester, Beauford: death of, 208; election of 1946, 192-195; election of 1948, 202; governor, 202-203, 203-208

Jim Wells County, voter irregularities in, 201

Joe Belden Poll (*see* Belden Poll)

Johns Hopkins Hospital, 170

Johnson, Cone: election of 1914, 45; J. E. Ferguson, 42-43; J. W. Bailey, 22-23; prohibition movement, 25-26

Johnson, Lyndon B., 176; election of 1941, 169-174; election of 1948, 196-202; election of 1954, 221; elected president, 228; elected vice-president, 224; president, 226-227; vice-president, 225

Johnson, R. M., election of 1914, 45

Joiner, Columbus Marion, East Texas Oil Field opened by, 126

Jones County, 213

Justin boots, 214

Kansas, 153, 175, 177

Kansas City Southern Railroad, use of diesel locomotives by, 9

Kelly Field: World War I aviation, 62-63; World War II aviation, 185

Kemp, Louis W., investigation of highway frauds, 107

Kennedy, Jacqueline, 227

Kennedy, John F.: assassination of, 226; election of 1960, 224

Kerens, Texas, 167

Kerrville, Texas, 84

Kirby, John H., lumbering interests of, 21

Knox, Frank, 183

Korean War, 215

Ku Klux Klan, 121, 186; election of 1924, 83, 85-86, 88-92; election of 1926, 111; election of

1928, 113; election of 1930, 123; ended by anti-mask law, 92, 105; enforcement of morality by, 76-77; opposition by Moody, 108; organization, 76

Labor unions, election of 1946, 194
Landrum, Lynn: on election of 1940, 165; on election of 1941, 171; on election of 1942, 177
Lanham, Fritz, election of 1941, 169
Lanham, S. W. T., 35; governor, 27-28
Lapham, John J., 14-15
Lapham, Lewis H., 14-15
Lawlessness (see also Martial law), in oil towns, 102, 127
Legislature: impeachment of J. E. Ferguson, 59; investigation of frauds in Mrs. Ferguson's administration, 106-107; investigation of prison conditions, 31-32; session of 1915, 47-48; session of 1917, 51-54, 59; session of 1919, 70-71; session of 1921, 83-84; session of 1923, 86-88; session of 1925, 92, 104-105; session of 1927, 111-112; session of 1929, 114-116; session of 1931, 125-126; session of 1932, 128; session of 1933, 132-136; session of 1935, 143-145; session of 1937, 150-151; session of 1939, 160-162; session of 1941, 167-172; session of 1947, 202-203; session of 1949, 203-208, 215; session of 1951, 215; session of 1953, 220-221; session of 1955, 221; session of 1959, 223; World War I measures of, 59-60
Liberty bonds, 65
Light Crust Doughboys, 153
Lima, Tony, 214
Limestone County, oil discovered in, 12, 100

Llano County, 213
Lobbying, 143; action on by legislature of 1957, 222-223
London, England, 36, 86
Lone Star Steel Company, 212
Long, Huey, 119, 175
Longview, Texas, industry at, 212
Looney, Ben F.: election of 1920, 79-81; stand on prohibition movement, 26
Louisiana, 3, 79
Love, Thomas B., election of 1930, 121-124
Love Field, World War I, 63
Lucas, Anthony B.: Gulf Oil Corporation, 13-14; oil discoveries of, 1-6
Lucas, Mrs. Anthony B., 2
Lucas No. 1 (see Spindletop)
Lubbock, Texas, as air training center in World War II, 185
Lubbock Avalanche-Journal, election of 1942, 179
Lufkin, Texas, 87
Luling, Texas, oil discovered at, 100
Lumbering, 213

MacCorkle, S. A., 230
MacIntosh, P. R., 103
Maedgen, C. E., 49
Magnolia Petroleum Company, organization of, 15
Manford, Durwood, 206
Mann, Gerald C., election of 1941, 171-174
Manufacturing (see Industry)
Marion County, 79
Martial law: as issue in election of 1932, 129; declared, 127
Mayer, Louie, 1-2
Mayfield, Earle B., 196; election of 1922, 85; election of 1928, 114; election of 1930, 120-124
McCamey, Texas, influence of oil on, 102-103
McCraw, William, election of 1930, 157-159

McDonald, C. C.: election of 1934, 139-141; prohibition movement, 25-26

McGregor, Texas, 78

McKay, S. S., 229

McKinley, William, 1

McLennan County, 79

Mechanized farming: during World War II, 187; introduced in West Texas, 96

Mellon, A. A., 13-14

Mellon, R. B., 13-14

Mellon, W. L., 14

Mexia, Texas: lawlessness at, 102; oil discovered at, 12, 100

Mexia Field, opened, 12, 100

Midland, Texas: as air training center in World War II, 185; influence of oil on, 102-103

Miller, Barry, election of 1930, 121

Mineral Wells, Texas, 37

Minimum Foundation Program (see also Education), 204

Mississippi, 17, 38

Missouri, 21, 22

Molyneaux, Peter, quoted on J. E. Ferguson, 142-143

Moody, Dan: as attorney general, 107; election of 1926, 108-111; election of 1928, 113-114; election of 1930, 121-122, 124; election of 1932, 129-130; election of 1941, 170; election of 1942, 177-181; election of 1946, 194; governor, 111-113, 114-116

Moore County, oil discovered in, 100-101

Morris, Charles H., 48

Morris, G. C., on taxes, 161-162, 168

Morris County, 212

Morton, Oliver, 34

Moscow, Texas, 57

Murphy, Audie, 184

Nacogdoches, Texas, 3, 136

National Aeronautics and Space Administration, location at Houston, 224

National Recovery Administration, 120

National Youth Administration, 120

Natural Gas (see Oil and Gas industry)

Navarro County, oil discovered in, 12

Neff, Pat, 111, 139, 158; early life of, 78-79; election of 1920, 77-82; election of 1922, 84-85; election of 1946, 194; governor, 83-84, 86-87; prison reform, 106

Negroes: effect on of Ku Klux Klan, 76-77; during Great Depression, 118; voting of, 31

Nelson, Hobart, proposal by for unicameral legislature, 150

Nevada, 42

New Deal, 137; efforts to end Great Depression, 119-120; opposition to by W. L. O'Daniel, 175

New Haven, Connecticut, 34

New Republic, quoted on election of 1942, 177

New York, 112

New York, New York, 37, 39, 90

New York Evening Post, quoted on election of 1932, 128-129

New York Times: on election of 1934, 138, 142; on Griffinhagen Report, 135-136

Nimitz, Chester W., 184

Nixon, Richard M., election of 1960, 224

Nixon v. Condon, 31

Nixon v. Herndon, 31

Nineteenth Amendment, passed, 71

Ninetieth Division: World War I, 61; World War II, 184

Nobles, M. C., founder of Amarillo Oil Company, 100

Nocona, Texas, 214

Nolte, Eugene, Jr., election of 1946, 195

North American Aviation plant, World War II, 186

North Carolina, 39

Nugent, Thomas L., election of 1894, 33

Oats, in West Texas, 96
O'Daniel, W. Lee, 139, 191; early life of, 153-155; election of 1938, 152-160; election of 1940, 163-166; election of 1941, 169-174; election of 1942, 176-181; election of 1946, 194; election of 1956, 222; governor, 160-163, 166-174; senator, 174-181, 195-197
O'Daniel, Mrs. W. Lee, 155-156
Odessa, Texas: chemical plant at, 212; influence of oil on, 102-103
Ohio, 153
Oil and Gas industry (*see also* names of individual companies): East Texas field opened, 126-127; Great Depression, 126-127; Gulf Coast discoveries, 1-13; major companies organized, 13-16; pipelines laid, 11-13, 103; refineries built, 11, 103-104, 210-212; search for market, 8-10; source of taxes, 71, 99, 104, 112, 125, 144; Spindletop Field opened, 1-8; transportation problems of, 11; West Texas discoveries, 100-103; World War II, 187
Oklahoma City, Oklahoma, 100
Old-age pensions: established, 145; political issue in 1936, 147-149; urged by O'Daniel, 156, 159, 161-172
Oldham County, 100
One Hundred Third Infantry Regiment, World War II, 184
One Hundred Twelfth Cavalry Division, World War II, 184
Orange, Texas, 171
Oswald, Lee Harvey, 227

Palestine, Texas, industry at, 213
Palo Duro Canyon, surveyed for oil, 100
Pampa, Texas, chemical plant at, 212
Pampa Field, opened, 101

Panama Canal, 18
Panhandle (*see* High Plains)
Panic of 1907, effects in Texas, 29
Pardons (*see also* Board of Pardons and Paroles): given by Mrs. Ferguson, 105-106; issue in election of 1926, 108; issue in election of 1934, 141-142
Paris, Texas, 204
Parr, Archie, supporter of J. E. Ferguson, 87-88
Party Loyalty Bill, veto of, 114
Pasotex Petroleum Company, construction of pipeline, 103-104
Patman, Wright, election of 1941, 169-171
Pearl Harbor, 182
Pearson, Drew, 200
Pecos, Texas, influence of oil on, 102-103
Peddy, George, election of 1948, 196-198
Peden, E. A., 65
Penitentiary, reform of, 31-32, 115-116
Petroleum (*see* Oil and Gas industry)
Petrolia Field, opened, 12
Phillips, Nelson, 25-26
Pilots (*see* Aviation)
Pipelines (*see also* Oil and Gas industry), construction of, 11-13, 103
Pittsburg, Texas, 48
Poindexter, William, election of 1920, 79
Political Action Committee, 194
Politics (*see* Elections, Legislature, Taxes, and names of individual politicians)
Polk County, 57
Poll tax, 30
Populist Party, 33
Port Arthur, Texas, refinery at, 15
Porter, Jack, election of 1948, 202
Potter County, oil discovered in, 100-101
Powell, Texas, oil discovered at, 12
Primary elections (*see also* Elec-

tions), Terrell Election Law, 30-31

Prison (*see* Penitentiary)

Prize fighting: banned, 33; legalized, 134

Prohibition: effected in Texas, 26-27, 60; election of 1911, 24-26; election of 1914, 44-46; election of 1916, 48-50; election of 1928, 113-114; election of 1930, 121; election of 1933, 134-136; election of 1934, 140; history of movement, 23-24; legislative session of 1935, 143-144; repealed, 145

Property taxes (*see also* Taxes), 28

Proration (*see also* Oil and Gas industry), established for oil industry, 127

Putnam, Frank, election of 1930, 121-124

Radio, election of 1938, 152-160

Railroad Commission: creation of, 37; regulation of petroleum industry, 127

Rainey, Homer Price: election of 1946, 191-195; fired as president of University of Texas, 191

Ranching (*see also* Agriculture): changes in the 1920's, 97-98; changes during World War II, 190

Randolph Field, World War II aviation, 185

Ranger, Texas, lawlessness at, 102

Ranger Field, opened, 100

Rankin, George, prohibition movement, 26

Rationing, World War II, 186

Rayburn, Sam, 33, 225; prohibition movement, 25-26

Reagan, John H., death of, 32-33

Reagan County, oil discovered in, 100

Reapportionment, 83

Red Cross, during World War I, 65, 72-73

Red River Validation Bill, vetoed, 114

Refineries (*see also* Oil and Gas industry), construction of, 12, 103-104, 210-212

Republic Iron and Steel Company, founded, 15

Republican Party: election of 1924, 91-92; election of 1928, 114; election of 1946, 195; election of 1952, 216-220; election of 1956, 220; election of 1960, 224; election of 1964, 228

Rich Field, World War I aviation, 63

Rister, Carl Coke, 230

Robertson, Felix D., election of 1922, 88-92

Robertson, Sam, election of 1932, 131

Robertson Insurance Law, 29

Rockefeller, John D., 8

Rocksprings, Texas, 204

Rogers, Fred S., election of 1922, 84-85

Roosevelt, Franklin D., 36, 39, 132, 137, 143, 146, 163, 171, 173, 180, 183, 193, 197, 199, 216

Roosevelt, Theodore, 18

Rose, Texas, campaign for W. L. O'Daniel, 159

Ruby, Jack, 227

Runoff primary, law enacted, 80

Rusk County, oil discovered in, 126

Russell, Richard, 217

Sadler, Jerry: election of 1940, 163-166; election of 1946, 192-194

Salado, Texas, 42

Sales tax (*see also* Taxes), 160-162; issue in election of 1934, 140, 142; issue in election of 1936, 147; proposed by legislature in 1937, 150; proposed by legislature in 1941, 167; pro-

State Superintendent of Public Instruction, 205
Steen, Ralph W., 229
Sterling, Ross: early life of, 121; election of 1930, 120-125; election of 1932, 128-132; election of 1934, 142; election of 1946, 194; governor, 125-128; reform of state administration, 135
Stevenson, Adlai: election of 1942, 217-220; election of 1956, 220
Stevenson, Coke: election of 1946, 194; election of 1948, 195-202; governor, 190-191
Still, Mrs. Rae Files, 206-207
Sulfur, taxation of, 125
Sulphur Springs, Texas, 84, 110, 171
Supreme Court (United States), election of 1948, 201-202

Taft, William H., 34
Taft-Hartley Law, issue in election of 1948, 198
Taliaferro Field, World War I aviation, 63
Taxes: gasoline, 99, 104, 112, 144; legislative session of 1919, 70-71; legislative session of 1941, 167-168; problem of, 27-28; sales, 132-133, 140, 142, 147, 150, 160-162, 167; studied by W. L. O'Daniel, 160; tobacco, 104, 125, 168; transactions, 161, 162, 164
Taylor, James E., 206; call for sales tax by, 167
Teacher Retirement System: authorization of, 150; establishment of, 151
Teachers (see also Education): certification requirements established for, 205-208; pay boosted for, 204-208
Temple, Texas, 42, 43, 50
Temple State Bank, 42, 49
Tenant farming: election of 1914, 43-44; laws concerning, 47
Tennessee, 38, 79

Terrell, Alexander W.: life of, 37; sponsor of election law, 30
Terrell, J. T., 135
Terrell Election Law, 24; amendments to, 30-31, 80; passage of, 30
Texarkana, Texas, 170
Texas A. & M. College, 38, 39
Texas and New Orleans Railroad, use of diesel locomotives, 9
Texas Bar Association, 77
Texas Centennial, 146
Texas City, Texas, 187
Texas Company, organization of, 11, 14-15
Texas Election Bureau, election of 1948, 200
Texas Fuel Company (see Texas Company)
Texas Highway Commission, 51, 113, 121, 130
Texas Instruments, 213
Texas Rangers: joined with Department of Public Safety, 144; need for increasing number of, 105; oil town lawlessness, 102
Texas Regulars, 193, 195
Texas Rehabilitation and Relief Commission, 134
Texas State Fair (1918), 60
Texas State Hospitals and Special Schools Board, creation of, 203
Texas Technological College, opening of, 99
Texas Weekly (magazine), 142-143; election of 1932, 128-129; support of sales tax, 133
Third Army, World War II, 184
Thirty-sixth Division: World War I, 61; World War II, 184
Thomason, Robert Ewing, election of 1920, 79-81
Thompson, Ernest O.: election of 1938, 157-159; election of 1940, 163-166
Thornton, William M., 52
Thurber, 82
Thurman, J. Strom, election of 1948, 202

Winkler County: oil discovered in, 102; pipeline laid in, 103-104
Winningham, George, quoted on election of 1940, 165-166
Winnsboro, Texas, 48
Wise County, 213
Wise Field, World War I aviation, 63
Witt, Edgar: election of 1932, 129; election of 1934, 139-141
Wolters, Jake, election of 1918, 69-70
Women, World War II, 186-187
Women's suffrage: World War I, 60; becomes law, 71
Woodruff, Grady, 135-136
Woodruff Bill, defeated, 136
Woods, L. A., opposition to Gilmer-Aikin plan, 205
Workman's Compensation Insurance plan, enacted, 150
Works Progress Administration, 120
World War I, 36, 139, 165; effect in Texas, 56-66, 72-74; fear of sabotage, 73-74; prohibition during, 26-27; issue in election of 1918, 68-70
World War II: effect in Texas, 182-190; issue in election of 1942, 176-178
Wortham Field, opened, 100

Yarborough, Ralph, 226; election of 1952, 216-218; election of 1954, 220-221; election of 1956, 222; election of 1957, 223
Yates County, oil discovered in, 102
Yates Field, opened, 126
Yoakum, Texas, schools in, 205-206
Yorktown, Texas, 130
Young, James, election of 1930, 121-124
Youth Development Council, created, 203

Zapata County, voter irregularities in, 201